Soundings

Issue 24

A market State?

EDITORS
Stuart Hall
Doreen Massey
Michael Rustin

ASSOCIATE EDITORS
Geoff Andrews
Sarah Benton
Sally Davison
Jonathan Rutherford

POETRY EDITOR
Carole Satyamurti

REVIEWS EDITORS
Becky Hall and
Christine Clegg

ART EDITOR
Tim Davison

EDITORIAL OFFICE
Lawrence & Wishart
99a Wallis Road
London E9 5LN

ADVERTISEMENTS
Write for information to
Soundings,
c/o Lawrence & Wishart

SUBSCRIPTIONS
2003 subscription rates are (for three issues):
UK: Institutions £70, Individuals £35
Rest of the world: Institutions £80, Individuals £45

Collection as a whole © Soundings 2003
Individual articles © the authors 2003

No article may be reproduced or transmitted by any means, electronic or mechanical, including photocopying, recording or any information storage and retrieval system, without the permission in writing of the publisher, editor or author

ISSN 1362 6620
ISBN 0 85315 981 5

Cover photograph © Tim Davison 2003

Printed in Great Britain by
Cambridge University Press, Cambridge

Soundings is published three times a year, in autumn, spring and summer by:
Soundings Ltd c/o Lawrence & Wishart,
99a Wallis Road, London E9 5LN.
Email: soundings@l-w-bks.demon.co.uk

Website: www.lwbooks.co.uk/sounding.html

CONTENTS

Notes on Contributors — v

Editorial: A market state? — 7
Sally Davison

New Labour's double-shuffle — 10
Stuart Hall

Public choice theory: enemy of democracy — 25
Alan Finlayson

PFI: The only show in town — 41
Jonathan Rutherford

Pensions of mass destruction — 55
Richard Minns

Social democracy in Britain and Europe — 62
Interview with Renzio Imbeni

Snatching defeat from the jaws of victory: Britain and the euro — 69
George Irvin

Notes from Palestine — 84
Adah Kay

Youth groups and the politics of time and space — 90
Nora Räthzel

Five Poems — 112
Lorna Dowell, Alice Beer, Martha Kapos,
Patrick Early, Patrick Hobbs

Veil of Influence: the legacy of John Rawls — 117
Michael Saward

———— Continued on next page ————

Continued from previous page

Christopher Hill: an appreciation 125
Nora Carlin

The making of political identity: Edward Thompson 131
and William Cobbett
Michael Rustin

NOTES ON CONTRIBUTORS

Geoff Andrews is an associate editor of *Soundings*.

Alice Beer was born and educated in Vienna. She has lived in this country since the German occupation, and started writing poems eleven years ago.

Norah Carlin until recently taught history at Middlesex University. She is the author of *The Causes of the English Civil War* (Blackwell, 1999), *The First English Revolution* (Bookmarks, 1985) and many articles on historical and Marxist topics.

Lorna Dowell has a background in social work and adult education, and is currently working on poetry project in schools and with diverse community groups, as part of a local laureateship in Surrey. Her first collection, *Wasps' Nest in Woman's Head*, was published in 2001.

Patrick Early is retired, having spent a lifetime overseas, working for the British Council. He now lives in London and the south of France. He has published poems in British, Irish, Brazilian and Yugoslav journals.

Alan Finlayson is a Lecturer in the Department of Politics and International Relations, University of Wales Swansea and author of *Making Sense of New Labour*, published by L&W in March 2003.

Stuart Hall is an editor of *Soundings*.

Patrick Hobbs made bread in a monastery, managed a bar, made furniture and ran an art gallery before chronic illness forced him to turn back to poetry. Many of his poems have been published.

Renzio Imbeni is a Vice-President of the European Parliament and an MEP for the Democratici di Sinistra (DS, Left Democrats), the largest successor party to the Italian Communist Party.

George Irvin teaches economics at ISS, The Hague and does research on globalisation and development-related issues.

Martha Kapos is an American living in London. In 2002, she was included in Carcanet's *Oxford Poetry* anthology. Her first collection, *My Nights in Cupid's Palace*, is published by Enitharmon.

Adah Kay is an academic, writer and activist who has recently been living in Palestine. Her book on Palestinian child prisoners (written with two colleagues) will be published by Pluto in 2004.

Richard Minns is the author of *Pension Funds and British Capitalism*, Heinemann, 1980, and *The Cold War in Welfare; Stock Markets versus Pensions*, Verso, 2001.

Nora Räthzel is a reader at the department of sociology, university of Umeå, Sweden. Her research deals with issues of racism, gender relations, class, youth and public space.

Michael Rustin is an editor of *Soundings*.

Jonathan Rutherford is lecturer in Media and Cultural Studies at Middlesex University and author of several books, including *The Art of Life* (2000) and *Young Britain* (1998). He is an associate editor of *Soundings*.

Michael Saward is Professor of Politics at the Open University.

EDITORIAL

A market state?

This issue goes to press a time when disillusionment with New Labour is greater than it has been at any time since Tony Blair became leader. Clearly the war in Iraq and its aftermath is a major factor in this, but we focus here on what we regard as the second major problem of New Labour - its strategic promotion of the market as the dominant means of organising all aspects of life.

We see the government's alliance with the US as being integral to its neoliberal vision; at every opportunity it aligns itself against European social democrats and alongside the right. Its support for US leadership in the world is premised on its sharing of American values. And this means not only that it backs the unilateral deployment of force by the powerful against the weak, it also (apparently) believes that social justice can be brought about by the spread of markets both globally and locally.

The third way, whose wake took place in July at the international progressive governance conference, based its claim to fame on the idea that it could somehow steer a middle course between the state and the market. Stuart Hall, in his article on New Labour's embrace of neoliberalism, begins the formulation of a different way of describing this position.

He describes New Labour as adopting a double strategy, in which they pursue a subordinate strategy that tackles the typical concerns of their voters - redistribution, public services, etc - while simultaneously pursuing much more vigorously their main agenda of promoting marketisation. He describes the genealogy of this strategy as owing something to Clinton and triangulation, but he also analyses it in terms of Antonio Gramsci's concept of transformism. This double strategy enables the government to retain (or at least it has done so until recently!) its traditional supporters while continuously working to institute a new - 'social democratic' - variant of neo-liberalism.

Alan Finlayson looks at the way in which public choice theory has been used as a strategy in this war of position between the public and private. Public choice theory, apparently a neutral and objective way of looking at decision-making, equates economic choice with choice in non-market areas such as voting or policy development. Alan shows how the adoption of this approach to politics has helped to undermine any idea of social or collective decision-making, and has encouraged the notion of all political choices being made by individuals on the same basis as consumers selecting goods. He also shows how management strategies based on this theory are in harmony with New Labour's general subordination of the political to the economic.

Jonathan Rutherford looks at the mechanics of the active construction of a market in an area that was previously regarded as lying within the sphere of the social - that of education. He shows how the government has promoted market infrastructure in this area, and the problems this brings for students and staff. This is part of Jonathan's wider project of looking at 'frontier markets' - places where the frontiers between the private and public sectors are being redefined. In this process new markets are created through disaggregating public sector services and then reintegrating them into the market as a series of commodities. We think this process is a major part of the global drive towards neoliberalism and plan to commission more work within this field.

The jettisoning of any social provision for pensions is something that the World Bank, amongst others, has been promoting for some time. Richard Minns puts forward a straightforward argument (but not one which the Bank seems willing to comprehend) that there is a fundamental incompatibility between the aims of financial institutions (to make a profit) and the social aim of providing welfare for pensioners. He argues that the disappearance of social funds into financial institutions is a victory for the market in a conflict about who controls the delivery of pensions, and who gets most out of it - the deliverers or the supposed beneficiaries.

Our interview with Renzo Imbeni, a leading member of Democratici di Sinistra (DS), the largest successor party to the Italian Communist Party, provokes some interesting comparisons between New Labour and his own party (which can be seen as sharing many characteristics with New Labour - including a commitment to modernisation and pragmatism). It seems that the DS are more willing to recognise that their pragmatism has not endeared them to the electorate, and to engage with at least some of the agenda of the social movements opposing the war and resisting neoliberal globalisation. This further illustrates the increasing distance between New Labour and other centre left parties in Europe, which was underlined in the government's recent rejection of the adoption of the euro, discussed by George Irvin in this issue. It appears that modernisation, which once placed the European project at its heart, now favours instead a US-style approach to 'flexibility', and rejects a social market approach.

Other articles this issue include Michael Saward's very useful account of the work of John Rawls, Adah Kay's notes from Palestine, Nora Räthzel's discussion of identity formation among marginalised young people in a German city, and two articles continuing our theme of revisiting socialist history - Nora Carlin on Christopher Hill, and Mike Rustin on the relationship between Edward Thompson and William Cobbett.

Not long before we went to press we were shocked to hear of Paul Hirst's death. Many *Soundings* editors and readers have had long and productive relationships with Paul, and we all bitterly mourn him. It seems almost impossible that someone so full of energy and projects should no longer be here. We regard him as an undervalued treasure of the British left, and an intellectual whose wide-ranging work will continue in its influence for many years. We will carry a fuller appreciation of his life and work in a future issue.

SD

New Labour's double-shuffle

Stuart Hall

Stuart Hall looks at key elements in New Labour's strategic adaptation of the neo-liberal agenda.

The Labour election victory in 1997 took place at a moment of great political opportunity. Thatcherism had been decisively rejected by the electorate. But 18 years of Thatcherite rule had radically altered the social, economic and political terrain in British society. There was therefore a fundamental choice of directions for the incoming government.

One was to offer an alternative radical strategy to Thatcherism, attuned to the shifts which had occurred in the 1970s and 1980s; with equal social and political depth, but based on radically different principles. Two basic calculations supported this view. What Thatcherism seemed to have ruled out was both another bout of Keynesian welfare-state social democracy, Wilsonian-style, and another instalment of old-style nationalisation. More significantly, Thatcherism had evolved not just an effective occupancy of power, but a broad hegemonic basis for its authority. This 'revolution' had deep philosophical foundations as well as an effective popular strategy. . It was grounded in a radical remodelling of state and economy and the 'colonising' of civil society by a new neo-liberal common-sense. Its effects were 'epochal' (i.e. defined a new political stage).

This was not likely to be reversed by a mere rotation of the electoral wheel of fortune. The historic opportunities for the left required bold, imaginative thinking and decisive action in the early stages of taking power, signalling a new direction. Critical to this was a 'transitional programme' - a few critical examples, popular but radical, like raising taxes to repair the destruction of the social fabric, a re-invention of the state education system and the reversal of the very unpopular privatisation of rail - to be introduced at once, chosen for their indicative significance.

As critics, we had concentrated on this Thatcherite reconstruction of the political/ideological terrain. On this, we were fundamentally right. But we may have underestimated the degree to which all this was itself related to much deeper global shifts - the new post-industrial society, the struggle by capital to restore its 'right to manage', the 'globalisation' of the international economy (which was its way out of that impasse), the technological revolution and the rise of a new individualism and the hegemony of neo-liberal free-market ideas. This was the sea-change which overtook the world in the 1970s. It still constitutes the 'horizon' which everybody - including the left - is required to address.

The other choice was, of course, to adapt to Thatcherite/neo-liberal terrain. There were plenty of indications that this would be New Labour's preferred direction: Peter Mandelson's book, for example, and the revisionist ideas peddled in this triumphalist phase by the New Labour intelligentsia -'differences between left and right are obsolete'; 'there is no alternative' (to neo-liberal globalisation); 'we have no objection to people becoming filthy rich' - provided clear evidence of the kind of re-thinking in progress in inner New Labour circles. Certainly one had no illusions about what 'taking power as New Labour and governing as New Labour' implied. Martin Jacques and I wrote an article for *The Observer* called 'Thatcherism With a Human Face?' on the Sunday before the 1997 election, which cast us irrevocably into outer political darkness. We knew that, once squandered, such a moment would be lost for many years, perhaps forever. We had a strong premonition that New Labour had already made strategic choices which put it irrevocably on the second track.

And so it turned out. In a profound sense, New Labour has adapted to neo-liberal terrain - *but in a significant and distinctive way*. Its critics are still not sufficiently clear about what the nature of that adaptation is. Its novelty - if not in terms of what it consists of, then in how the elements are combined - is not well understood. Still, it took only a few weeks in 1997 for the basic direction to become crystal clear: the fatal decision to follow Conservative spending priorities and commitments, the sneering renunciation of redistribution ('tax and spend!'), the demonisation of its critics ('Old Labour!'), the new ethos of managerial authoritarianism ('We know that we are right'), the quasi-religious air of righteous conviction ('Either for us or against us'), the reversal of the historic commitment to equality, universality and collective social provision.

The welfare state had been Labour's greatest achievement, then savaged and weakened under Mrs Thatcher. Its de-construction was to be New Labour's historic mission. The two-tier society, corporate greed and the privatisation of need were inevitable corollaries. This was glossed positively as 'modernisation!' Who could possibly be against it? The linguistic operation - generating a veritable flowering of Third Way waffle, double-talk, evasions and 'spin', depending on which audience was being addressed - was critical to the whole venture.

The Prime Minister's recent claims that New Labour's reforms of schools and hospitals (i.e. the re-introduction of selectivity and creeping privatisation) are 'firmly within Labour's historic battle for social justice', or that foundation hospitals are fully in line with the efforts of Nye Bevan to create a universal NHS which would de-commodify health care - that such hospitals are *really* designed to 'give power back to local communities' rather than to open the door to private investment - are only the most recent, blatant examples. The shamelessness of this widespread evasiveness - being economical with the truth as a principle of government - and the profound contempt for the electorate it implies, has gone far to corrupt the whole political culture. Cynicism and political apathy have inevitably followed. (New Labour 'spin' has it that falling electoral participation is a sign of mass contentment. But what is the point of voting, if the result is a New Labour administration which agrees with the Tories on fundamentals, *only with bells on?*)

New Labour does have a long-term strategy, 'a project': what Antonio Gramsci called the 'transformism' of social democracy into a *particular variant* of free-market neo-liberalism. However, it remains fashionable to deny that anything like a project is at work here. Even the disenchanted cling desperately to the hope that English pragmatism will prevail. New Labour's reasoned critics - Roy Hattersley, Frank Dobson, Chris Smith, Bill Morris, even Polly Toynbee - remain 'loyal' (but to what?). They look hopefully for signs that New Labour will of its own accord - now that the second term is spinning out of control, perhaps in the third? - refashion itself into something different. The key thing to say about New Labour is that its so-called 'pragmatism' is the English face it is obliged to wear in order to 'govern' in one set of interests while maintaining electoral support in another. It isn't fundamentally pragmatic, any more than Thatcherism was - which doesn't mean that it isn't constantly making things up on the run. In relation to the NHS, Mrs Thatcher too was pragmatic in the short run ('The NHS is safe in our hands!'), but strategically an anti-pragmatist. As with the miners, she knew when to withdraw in order to fight again, more effectively, another day.

Pragmatism is the crafty, incremental implementation of a strategic programme - being flexible about the way you push it through, giving ground when the opposition is hot, tactically revising your formulations when necessary. (Having given us 'the enabling state' and the celebration of 'risk', the distinguished Third Way guru Anthony Giddens now effortlessly slips us on to 'the ensuring state' - as more businesses absolve themselves of their pensions obligations.) It requires modestly shifting the emphases to catch the current political wind, saying what will keep traditional 'heartland' supporters happy ('It can come across a bit technocratic, a bit managerial' - the P.M.), whilst always returning to an inflexible ideological base-line ('the fundamental direction in which we are leading the country is correct' - the P.M.). Of course, there will be a thousand scams and devices dreamed up by New Labour's blue-skies policy-wonks, as 'government is re-invented' - for that is the mission of the policy-advisers-turned-civil-servants in the No.10 policy, strategy and innovation units, and the New Labour-inclined 'think-tanks' (the IPPR, Demos). But unerringly, at the strategic level, the project returns to its watch-words: 'wealth-creation', 'reform' and 'modernisation'.

There is *a dominant strategy or logic* at work here, and fundamentally it is *neo-liberal* in character. Thus New Labour has worked - both domestically and globally (through the institutions of 'global governance' such as the IMF, the WTO, the World Bank, etc) - to set the corporate economy free, securing the conditions necessary for its effective operation at home and globally. It has renounced the attempts to graft wider social goals on to the corporate world. (Will Hutton's project of 'stake-holder power' lasted all of five minutes.) It has de-regulated labour and other markets, maintained restrictive trade union legislation, and established relatively weak and compliant regulatory regimes. The Rail regulator, for example, cuts train services and raises fares in order to make rail more 'efficient' (!) It mainly serves as the conduit for substantial public subsidies to inefficient private firms, taking the risk out of investment, but still cannot find a public alternative to the railways' fragmented structure. The new Broadcasting regulator's main purpose seems to be to dismantle the barriers which currently prevent global interests like Murdoch buying at will into and monopolising British press and media channels.

New Labour has spread the gospel of 'market fundamentalism' - markets and market criteria as the true measure of value - far and wide. It has 'cosied up to business', favouring its interests in multiple public and private ways (from the Formula One cigarette advertising scandal onwards). The trend to inequality has grown exponentially during its administrations, escalating towards American proportions. 'The rich now have a bigger share of the nation's post-tax income than at any time under Mrs Thatcher' (Michael Meacher). It has protected corporate boardroom greed; and promoted business influence in shaping social agendas favourable to its interests at the heart of government (the connections of those advising the government on GM and environmental issues with pharmaceutical and bio-technology corporate interests have only just come to light). It has promoted the image of 'the businessman' and 'the entrepreneur' as *the* principal social role model, spreading the gospel of 'entrepreneurial values' ('efficiency', 'choice', 'selectivity') through the land. It has pursued a splendidly variable range of privatisations - sustaining the sell-off of critical public assets (transport, the London tube, air-traffic control, the postal services), forcing the public sector to 'mimic' the market in its internal operations, fatally blurring the public/private distinction (Public Finance Initiatives, public-private 'partnerships') and stealthily opening doors for private investment in, and the corporate penetration of, parts of the public sector (the prison service, schools, the NHS). Every media debate as to whether the latest creeping privatisation is '*really*' privatisation' is a form of trivial pursuit.

However, New Labour has adapted the fundamental neo-liberal programme to suit its conditions of governance - that of a social democratic government trying to govern in a neo-liberal direction while maintaining its traditional working-class and public-sector middle-class support, with all the compromises and confusions that entails. It has modified the classic anti-statist stance of American-style neo-liberalism by a 're-invention of active government'. This is not a return to government as we have known it, but a revolution in 'governance' (see the 1999 *Modernizing Government* White Paper). The term 'governance' is itself another shifty New Labour concept: not a synonym for 'government' but the signifier of 'a new process of governing, a changed condition of ordered rule', specifically designed to blur the difference between state and civil society (Rhodes 1996). As Paul Du Gay argues, this involves 'a new rationality of rule', in which 'political government has been re-structured in the name of an economizing logic'.

'Entrepreneurial governance', its advocates advise, promotes competition between service providers, favours the shift from bureaucracy to 'community', focuses not on inputs but on outcomes (delivery), redefines clients as consumers, de-centralises authority through 'participatory management', and prefers market mechanisms to administrative ones (Osborn and Gaebler, quoted in Du Gay, p13). Its neo-liberal origins are hard to disguise. Far from breaking with neo-liberalism, 'entrepreneurial governance' constitutes its continuation - but in a transformed way. 'To govern better the state is to govern less but more "entrepreneurially"' (Du Gay).

The entrenched New Labour orthodoxy is that only the private sector is 'efficient' in a measurable way. The public sector is, by definition, 'inefficient' and out of date, partly because it has social objectives beyond economic efficiency and value-for-money. It can only save itself by becoming more like the market. This is the true meaning of 'modernisation'. As Alan Finlayson argues, 'Modernisation' is a loosely performative speech-act, in the sense that it 'acquires meaning and force only in the moment of its usage … It is an "up" word, that makes things sound exciting, progressive and positive … [Its] usage helps generate an appearance of structured and unified thinking … It helps to render "natural" and un-contestable that which is not necessarily so'.[1]

Part of its purpose is to establish a permanent divide between new sheep and old goats. Public sector workers who oppose this drift are represented as immured in the past, seriously 'out of date' and therefore 'the enemy within'. They too must be 'modernised'. Of course, in fact they are grossly under-rewarded in relation to the private sector, and deeply excluded as partners in the drive to improve the services they actually deliver - the objects, but never the subjects, of 'reform'. The Prime Minister advised them to think of themselves more as 'social entrepreneurs'! Meanwhile, the whole concept of 'the public interest' and 'the public good' has collapsed. It too has been declared obsolete.

---

1. Alan Finlayson, *Making Sense of New Labour*, L&W 2003, p67.

New Labour's critics on the left or media commentators are too embarrassed to invoke it. The proposition that markets are the only measure of 'the social good' - advanced by Hayek, adopted by Mrs Thatcher and reinvented by New Labour - has been swallowed, hook, line and sinker. Marketisation is now installed in every sphere of government. This silent revolution in 'governance' seamlessly connects Thatcherism to New Labour. It is the code which underpins the 'jargon' which New Labour ministers spout in their sleep. It is uttered as 'truth' by New Labour's welfare intellectuals from the hallowed walls of places like the LSE.

The new managerialism

During the 1980s, sceptical critics used to ask how the analysis of Thatcherite ideology affected 'the real world'. One answer then - and it is now even more the case - is through the practices of management. Apparently simply a neutral social technology, 'The New Managerialism' is really the vehicle by means of which neo-liberal ideas actually inform institutional practices. In New Labour's case, in the public sector, this is via the so-called New Public Management approach. This involves the marketisation of the state's governing and administrative practices, the transformation of public service individuals into 'entrepreneurial subjects' and the adaptation of the machinery of state to the 'mission' of 'entrepreneurial governance'. Central to this reconstruction of governance and the state is the enthusiastic adoption of a 'Public Choice' approach to the public sector. This 'shift[s] the balance of incentives [from input to delivery, and] ... in Britain in the 1980s led to the contracting out of services, the spread of internal markets and outright privatisation' (Finlayson, 111). It is the main source of the drive to re-constitute citizens as consumers.[2]

To its influence we now owe the boring repetition of 'choice' as one of the key 'modern' values in Tony Blair's discourse. Actually, there is no identified groundswell of public demand for more 'choice' in the abstract. Undoubtedly, many people would quite like to be able to choose a good secondary school for their children and an efficient hospital to be ill in, wherever they live and however rich or poor they may be - a quite different matter. However, repeating that 'choice' is a wide-spread demand is a way of making what is affirmed as a fact but is really only a prophecy, self-fulfilling, on the principle that 'those things

---

2. For a critique, see Catherine Needham's pamphlet, *Citizen-Consumers*, Catalyst 2003.

which people can be made to believe are true will be 'true' (i.e. 'real') in their effects'. As The Prime Minister said, in a classic instance of Third Way gobble-de-gook, 'Choice enhances quality of provision for the poorest, helping to tackle inequalities while it also strengthens middle class commitment to collective provision' (*The Courage of Our Convictions*, 2002, p28). He added that the purpose of public service reform was 'to deliver in a modern, consumer-focused fashion'. As Catherine Needham rightly observed, 'ministers have begun to step back from the explicit language of consumerism and competition, while still continuing to endorse the principles behind them' (*Citizen-Consumers*, p25).

> 'the silent revolution in "governance" seamlessly connects Thatcherism to New Labour'

The New Public Management 'empowers' civil servants to abandon the principles of political impartiality and, like private-sector CEOs, 'take ownership' of their sectors, in a more 'agency-driven' style (the doctrine embodied in the famous 'Next Steps' document). It replaces professional judgement and control by the wholesale importation of micro-management practices of audit, inspection, monitoring, efficiency and value-for money, despite the fact that neither their public role nor their public interest objectives can be adequately re-framed in this way. For this purpose, we require an army of managers, who know little of the content of their field, but everything about strategies of managerial control - and a regiment of consultants to advise clients how to 'creatively' fudge their monitors. More widely, it fosters the concerted drive to introduce corporate business leaders into every sector of public life in order to spread a climate favourable to 'entrepreneurialism'. As the private corporations and advisers on loan from business become more and more practically entrenched at the centre of government, and their representatives actively 'volunteered' at more local levels, so 'the corporate enterprise' itself becomes progressively *the new model of the state* ...

The state's 'educative' function combines intensive micro-management and centralisation of targets with more strategic interventions exercised 'culturally' and 'at a distance'. The latter is a neo-Foucauldian, 'governmentality' approach - controlling behaviour and outcomes not by direct constraints but through the consent and 'freedom' of individuals (which may explain why neo-Foucauldians like Nikolas Rose are so favourably mesmerised by it!) This approach does not require a mass conversion to entrepreneurial values (another error made by our critics in the 1980s). Instead, knowing that individuals can occupy various subject positions, the New Managerialism aims to re-produce all of us in the new position of practising 'entrepreneurial subjects', by fostering certain 'capacities' while down-grading others, shifting individual behaviour indirectly by altering the environment in which people work, and operationalising *new values* by 'modernising' *old practices*. You change what individuals do not by changing their minds but by changing their practices, and thus the 'culture'.

The wider point is to inculcate in the population at large a new *habitus* ('culture-change'): making into a new kind of common sense those habits and practices which the new 'free-market', consumer-focused conception of 'governance' requires. This approach is effective well outside the machinery of state. Slowly but surely, everybody - even if kicking and screaming to the end - becomes his/her own kind of 'manager'. The market and market criteria become entrenched as the *modus operandi* of 'governance' and institutional life. Media commentators and the press know no other language with which to address public issues. They may object to this or that piece of New Labour over-centralised 'managerialism', but seem unable to place the *logic* from which these arise. Democracy has long since faded as a practical ideal. Except in the banal form of 'liberal-democracy', Tony Blair has not had a single thought on the subject over two terms in government. The general public seems to have swallowed this managerialist discourse whole.

The passing-off of market fundamentalism as 'the new common sense' has helped to drive home the critical lesson which underpins the 'reform' of the welfare state: the role of the state 'nowadays' is not to support the less fortunate or powerful in a society which 'naturally' produces huge inequalities of wealth, power and opportunity, but to help individuals *themselves to provide* for all their social needs - health, education, environmental, travel, housing, parenting, security in unemployment, pensions in old age, etc. Those who can - the new middle-class majority - must. The rest - the residuum - must be 'targeted', means-tested, and kept to a minimum of provision lest the burden threaten 'wealth creation'. This is what we used to call 'the one third/two thirds strategy', and is now referred to as 'the two-tier society'. New Labour, of course, says it cannot recognise the phenomenon. However, it is manifestly the lynchpin of public sector 'modernisation'. It sounds the death-knell to the old notion of 'the public realm', the social conception of the individual ('There is no such thing as society') and the basic social-democratic idea of collective provision.

A double regime

New Labour is therefore confusing in the signals it gives off, and difficult to characterise as a regime. It constantly speaks with forked tongue. It *combines* economic neo-liberalism with a commitment to 'active government'. More significantly, its grim alignment with the broad global interests and values of corporate capital and power - the neo-liberal project, which is in the *leading position* in its political repertoire - is paralleled by another, *subaltern* programme, of a more social-democratic kind, running alongside. This is what people invoke when they insist, defensively, that New Labour is not, after all, 'neo-liberal'. The fact is that New Labour is a *hybrid* regime, composed of two strands. However, one strand - the neo-liberal - is in the dominant position. The other strand - the social democratic - is subordinate. What's more, its hybrid character is not simply a static formation; it is the *process* which combines the two elements which matters. The process is 'transformist'. The latter always remains subordinate to and dependent on the former, and is *constantly being 'transformed' into* the former, dominant one.

How can we explain New Labour's double character? The political scientist Andrew Gamble long ago pointed out that left parties in government are often subject to contrary pulls - one towards realising their governmental programme, the other towards doing what is necessary to win electoral support and hold on to power. These frequently conflict. New Labour's subaltern programme is driven by the second of those imperatives. It is the necessary 'cost' of maintaining loyalty amongst its traditional supporters, whilst its governmental project favours a quite different set of interests. This is not necessarily just opportunistic calculation. Many Labour MPs have persuaded themselves that New Labour is still fundamentally attached to 'old' Labour values, which will somehow eventually reassert themselves; and the Blair government itself defends its massive departures from these old values by rhetorically 'spinning' its verbal continuity with them. It must therefore find space in its programme to address these subordinate pressures and constituencies - provided they are not allowed to de-rail the progress towards a more developed market state. Thus New Labour's 'balancing act', its two-step shuffle - and the way it has become mired in endless

19

'spin' in order to square the impossible circle.

There is another consideration. The full-blown neo-liberal drive to the market state we saw in Thatcherism had its costs. Its brutalism antagonised many in society, including some of its original supporters. People thought neo-liberalism 'red in tooth and claw' a step too far. Even many of Mrs T's most fervent converts eventually abandoned her for reasons of electoral calculation. But moving to the full blown market state via a subordinated social-democratic route has the advantage of addressing some of the problems of 'the residuals' and losers - those who are likely to benefit least from the neo-liberal route. It also takes account of some of the 'costs' and the social upheaval which its 'trans-formism' will create. It is authentically a 'hegemonic' strategy, even though it may not be capable of producing a stable hegemonic outcome. It aims to win enough consent as it goes, and to build subordinate demands back into its dominant logic. Forging a plausible or pragmatic pathway from left to right, carrying a proportion of its old supporters with it on particular points, dividing and confusing the oppositions, and winning a measure of consent for the project, may serve to establish neo-liberal society on firmer, less contested foundations. Certainly, the confusion which its double-headed strategy sows in its own ranks obscures the long-term objective and prevents a coherent and organised opposition from emerging. The social-democratic route to neo-liberalism may turn out in the end to be what Lenin might have called 'the best shell' for global capitalism.

The subordinate part of the New Labour programme involves a certain measure of indirect taxation and redistribution, reforms like the minimum wage, family tax credits, inducements to return to work (the high visibility given to 'skills and training', however, is solidly in line with the neo-liberal emphasis on 'the supply side'). To this we also owe, in the second term, the build up of concern about the delivery of public services, including a substantial injection of public funds into health and education. In a retrospective gloss, New Labour now suggests that the latter was always what it intended for its second term, but the evidence for this is not compelling. In its first term it systematically demonised the public sector and redistribution, and was consistently and unapologetically 'entrepreneurial'. Failing public services surfaced as an issue, unannounced and unanticipated, towards the end of the first term, around the time of the resignation of Peter Kilfoyle, when the disillusionment amongst New Labour's 'heartland' traditional supporters had reached fever pitch; it was clearly forced on to New Labour's political agenda from the outside.

Public service delivery in the second term is really the key to understanding how this *hybrid* New Labour regime functions. New Labour is committed to improving the delivery of public services. But its means of achieving this are impeccably 'new managerialist'. Redistribution, where it occurs, must be by stealth, lest a more vocal and organised constituency should develop around it. New Labour has set its stony face against enlisting public service workers and professionals in the enterprise. It refuses to countenance a return to a more full-blooded 'mixed' public/private regime (hence the unrelenting vendetta against Ken Livingstone about funding the tube). Instead, it has adopted the top-down managerialist approach of centralised control, supplemented by the rich panoply of 'the audit culture': the exponential expansion of public service managers over professionals at the coal face; unachievable targets; socially uninformative league tables; perpetual monitoring; moralistic 'shaming'; the merciless proliferation of pointless bureaucratic detail; the introduction of selectivity under the guise of 'diversity' (another piece of linguistic expropriation); vulgar hectoring by public sector ministers re-trained in the new, 'bruiser school' of New Labour leadership (Prescott, Blunkett, Clarke, Reid); and the novel, contradictory strategy of 'tough love'.

In public service 'reform', how does the articulation of the subaltern 'social democratic' part of the repertoire with the dominant, neo-liberal part operate? Every change in the public sector *must* be accompanied by a further tightening of the 'modernising' screw, as the unshakeable *trade-off of a certain kind of 'reform'*. The public think the aim here is 'better delivery'. The government knows that the price which must be paid for this is 'more modernisation'. Nothing - however good or necessary - is allowed to happen which is not accompanied by another dose of 'reform'. And the kind of 'reform' implied must meet the following criteria: (a) it must open the door to private investment or blur the public/private distinction; (b) it must meet market criteria of efficiency and value-for-money; (c) it must put managerial authority in command; (d) it must reform working practices in a less collective, more individualised direction; (e) it must stimulate competition and divide workers by introducing incentive pay schemes and undermining collective bargaining; (f) it must weaken the bargaining power of the unions; (g) it must reduce the size of the workforce and the cost of the service; (h) it must hold public sector pay in line well behind the private sector; (i) the service must be remodelled along 'two-tier' lines by introducing selectivity. In short, marketisation and privatisation, whether frontally or incrementally introduced, is what 'reform' now *means*. This type of 'modernisation' is the New Labour 'trade-off' for any kind of change.

Take the fire-fighters' dispute. Of course, a modern fire service should function efficiently. Fire-fighters deserve to be well paid for the risks they take on our behalf, and in return should have their paramedical skills and professional levels enhanced. 'Spanish practices', where they exist, serve no useful social purpose. But New Labour is determined that they should not get a penny more unless and until they first submit to new forms of managerial control imposed from above, and at the cost of cuts in the labour force and the number of fire stations.

New Labour 'hybridisation' has its political antecedents. Its immediate ancestor is Clintonian triangulation. Clinton borrowed from the Democrats, borrowed from the Republicans, and moved the whole wagon-train further towards the market - a 'knight's move', or three-pronged shift, which was very influential in New Labour thinking in its early stages, and even more so when Clinton was able to bring off the much-envied prize of a second election victory. The essence of this 'transformism' game depends on pulling selectively, and in an ordered hierarchy, from opposing political repertoires, maintaining a double-address to their different 'publics', so that you can advance a 'radical' (sic) overall strategy of governance, on the one hand, *while maintaining electoral support and securing a third term on the other*. The subordinate agenda - redistribution, belated public investment, public service 'delivery', etc - has to do, essentially, with this second goal. That is the crucial 'double-shuffle' or 'triple-play' involved in the New Labour project. It delivers what Philip Bobbit calls 'the market state', or, more simply, a *'social democratic variant of neo-liberalism'* (in exactly the same way that Thatcherism delivered a 'neo-liberal variant' of classic Conservatism). No prizes for identifying the common thread!

This is the principal reason why 'spin' is an essential and organic part of the New Labour project; it is not a surface excrescence, as many critics fondly suppose. 'Spin' has the obvious purpose of putting a favourable gloss on everything. It turns every argument, by a rhetorical sleight-of-hand, in New Labour's favour. It is a sign of the reduction of politics to public relations and the manipulation of public opinion. But 'spin' also has the much deeper function of 'squaring circles': re-presenting a broadly neo-liberal project, favourable to the global interests of corporate capital and the rich, in such a way that it can mobilise the popular consent of Labour voters and supporters, the trades unions and the less-well-off in society. This sleight-of-hand can only be done by continuously *sliding* one agenda into or underneath another. The New Labour phenomenon of linguistic slippage is thus a function of its double-pronged mode of address. It spins the word 'reform', with its positive associations - the Reform Acts, the Factory Acts, the welfare state, etc - until it somehow becomes equivalent to its absolute opposite - marketisation! It masks the consistent shift of direction from public to private, by exploiting the vagaries of words like 'change' - or 'radical' - which can point in any direction (after all, even Mussolini made the trains run on time!). Choice, which is designed to introduce selectivity and the private sector, is represented as part of an anti-inequality strategy. 'Spin' mobilises a concept's positive resonances - and transfers this charge to a very different, usually contrary, idea.

Take the NHS. It remains 'free at the point of delivery' (actually, it isn't, but let that pass for a moment). Of course some public hospitals will now be built by private construction companies on PFI terms, whose real costs will only become clear two or three generations ahead; and some of its services will be delivered by private American or British pharmaceutical or health service companies to foundation hospitals which have been 'freed' to raise funds and compete for staff. Who cares that this is all at the expense of the general social provision of health care and the founding principle of universality, and will create a two-tier service? You foreground the pragmatic practicalities of 'delivery' in order to silence these other awkward questions about principle and purpose you would prefer not to have to answer. What 'delivery' presumes is that no-one any longer *cares* who owns, runs, controls or profits from, health-care, providing the possessively-individual consumer's personal need is satisfied. The reduction of the citizen to consumer, and the 'privatisation of need' at the centre of the market model, are thus the absolutely crucial but unspoken foundations to this strategy. New Labour not only banks on the fact that this shift has occurred, but is actively 'spinning' to bring it about. It is not a passive victim of sociological change but an active agent in its unravelling. If people think of themselves as having a stake in the NHS, then it matters to them who owns it, what principles inform its operation. But if they can be induced, by relentless 'spin', to think of the NHS only in the individualist terms of 'I need a better bed', or 'I need to move faster up the waiting list', then they won't mind who produces it or whether health becomes a lucrative site of private sector investment. It's simply one more 'market' response to consumer demand.

At the moment, the resistance to the New Labour project is coming mainly from the backwash of the invasion of Iraq and Blair's decision to commit Britain, wholesale and without qualification, as an ancillary support to the US drive to global hegemony. No account of the New Labour project would be complete without taking into account how its domestic programme fits into its global mission to push through a global neo-liberal agenda, and the dependency this has produced in the foreign policy and geo-political domains. The account offered here is therefore incomplete. However, it does have a political purpose. The New Labour 'project' is a complex political initiative and we need to understand its complexities better than we do. The idea that it has simply, like Topsy, grown higgledy-piggledy by its own accord, is nonsense. Now that there are serious forces wishing to distance themselves from the overall goals, we need to build the different, particular points of opposition (the war, the US alliance, foundation hospitals, selectivity in education, private-public initiatives, the reconstruction of the NHS, the trade union opposition to privatisation, etc) into a more substantive and integrated critique, in order that a more concerted and coherent vision - and the political forces to make it popular and put it into effect - can emerge. The two years between now and the next election are just enough time to construct an alternative political project for/from the left. Failing this, beyond the election awaits a third installation of New Labour's double shuffle, or - Heaven forfend - IDS!

Public choice theory: enemy of democracy

Alan Finlayson

Alan Finlayson looks at current arguments about depoliticisation, and the contribution that public choice theory, and the wider New Labour tendency to privilege the economic over the political, has made to this process.

Politics is a highly contestable concept. One of the most important things any ideology has to do is establish a particular definition of what politics is, and thus of what it is for. This limits the scope of potential challenges and provides a kind of legitimacy to a political position, in as much as it can be believed to derive from certain social facts. Political theories are thus always also social theories of some kind. They posit something (or some set of things) as given, as the basic features of social life. From this it follows that politics is there to do certain sorts of things. Actions or aspirations that fall outside of this definition are considered non-political, beyond the scope of political action, or just not possible.

There is one particularly important aspect to this, central to any 'ontology' of the political: the relationship between politics and economics. A crucial question to ask of any political outlook is, does it conceive of politics as an activity that can act on economics or as one that is only acted upon by economic forces? New Labour's claims about a new society and economy, about modernisation, necessitate a call for a new politics. We have to ask, therefore, whether or not they conceive of this politics as superior or subordinate to the new economy.

This extract seeks to explicate this aspect of the underlying political 'ontology' of New Labour, and to understand what its implications are for democratic politics. It will pay particular attention to the ways in which public choice theory feeds into an 'economic' view of society and politics, and at how this in turn creates the conditions for a further general depoliticisation.

Politics and economics

In feudal systems, the arrangement of political power amongst Lords related directly to their control of land, the primary economic resource. Economic and political structures were entwined. But it is a founding principle of capitalist states that political and economic structures should be separate. This imagined division has carried on into everyday thinking, especially in the academy. Much of the time the two fields of politics and economics are presumed to carry on with quite separate theoretical frameworks and analytical tools, as if they are analysing totally distinct forms of human behaviour. Where there has been a recent intellectual relationship between economics and politics, in rational and public choice theories for example, it has taken the form of a colonisation of one by the other. But the 'spheres' of economics and politics are both spheres of social power; they are intimately related and in the form of the state find their most clearly unified expression. The state is an instrument for the control of both economics and politics and battles fought over the state can sometimes be understood as battles over what should be dominant and what should be marginalised. A central aspect of contemporary ideological struggle is conflict over the extent to which emerging and expanding economic forces can in fact be controlled by any state structure.

New Labour does not in general formulate political ideas on the basis of a substantial moral claim about the nature of society and the distribution of its resources. It does so on the basis of a 'sociological' claim about the novel condition of contemporary society; a belief that the world has been transformed, while our political ideas have not kept up the pace. For this reason it constantly returns to the need to adapt to existing economic circumstances. As Blair puts it in his explanation of The Third Way: 'Just as economic and social change were critical to sweeping the Right to power, so they were critical to its undoing. The challenge for the Third Way is to engage fully with the implications of that change'. The Third Way response is to aim for a 'dynamic knowledge-based economy founded on individual empowerment and opportunity, where governments enable, not command, and the power of the market is harnessed to serve the public interest'. This does mean that a need for the reinvigoration of civil society and international co-operation is recognised.[1] But these are understood as necessary supports for the effective functioning of the economy, rather than as goals in themselves.

The decline of politics

There are well established arguments accounting for the decline of politics. For example, it could be argued that we are experiencing the fallout of the transition to what Colin Crouch has called 'post-democracy'.[2] We have passed through the great era of democratic expansion when mass society produced mass parties able to, approximately, represent the interests of their mass memberships and struggle for control and influence of the institutions of state. Now we in the 'old' democracies are bored by it all. Politicians are not well regarded by the populations that choose them. Declining faith in the competence of government is matched only by the conviction that it can't do anything anyway.

We once had the idea that democracy, in allowing wide-ranging and unrestricted discussion, would enable an enlightened public to reach more rational decisions. Individual rights to free speech and association, protection from harm and the ensuring of a minimum of harassment made it possible for a people collectively to address themselves, develop their values and opinions and express them. But who, any more, believes that such a public sphere exists? Where are the media through which such a discussion can take place? Today there are few ways in which the people can discuss issues, in an open-ended and inclusive way, let alone in a manner that transforms the

---

1. Tony Blair, *The Third Way: New Politics for a New Century*, Fabian Society 1998, pp6-7.
2. Colin Crouch, *Coping with Post-democracy*, Fabian Society 2000.

perspectives and understanding of the participants. But even if they could, it is no longer clear, and never really was, who 'the people' are. If it is admitted that the people are not an already unified collective but a collection of disparate and mobile groups with differing and contradictory interests, the whole abstraction begins to break down. Treating the social world as fractured only by mass classes allowed a holding pattern to emerge in which mass parties could represent (or fight over) class interests. But it seems now as if such notions of collective unity, whether national or class, were always myths. Society is so clearly fractured along lines of region, occupation, ethnicity, gender and so on, that the constitution of them as a 'people' capable of speaking with, to and for each other is no longer desirable, or at least requires greater resources of political imagination than we currently have.

Meanwhile, many of the problems to which we want solutions cannot, it seems, be resolved at a national level. To function, democracies have required not only meaningful discussion and a sense of the collective will, but a clear and authoritative body to whom that will could be expressed and so acted upon. But, as governments and numerous pundits never tire of telling us, national states no longer have the power to act on all of such collective decisions. The global firm can exercise power over national governments and effectively force them to concede to it in certain areas of fiscal and employment policy. Under the influence of neo-liberal ideology, the British government has withdrawn from many areas of what was once public provision and seems, as Crouch argues, to have lost confidence in itself as a provider of anything. Unsurprisingly, the public has lost confidence too. Subject to the influences of a powerful global corporate elite, government finds it even harder to pretend that it represents collective interests, and the cycle of disaffection extends itself (Crouch, pp22-36).

But - and this is a crucial point that is not taken on board by New Labour - this process should not be understood simply as an inevitable development deriving from fixed tendencies in social organisation. It is made possible by such processes, but entrenched by political decisions, values and ideologies. But New Labour's in-built tendency to regard the political as secondary to the economic means that it often overlooks this side of the process. And all this has been greatly reinforced by the arrival of public choice theory on to the political scene.

Public choice theory

'Public choice theory' and other 'economic' theories of democracy, while they originated earlier in the twentieth century, took off in the 1970s and 1980s. Such apparently arcane 'academic' theses can have an influence that is almost impossible to measure, for they are disseminated through leading universities and institutes (such as Nuffield College in the UK) to politicians, civil servants and opinion formers. Such theories usually consider themselves to be neutral and objective methods of political study, and they are incapable of conceiving of their own capacity to create the very conditions they purport merely to describe. But, as Colin Hay trenchantly argues, with regard to Anthony Downs' theories of electoral competition: 'New Labour has learned to play the "politics of catch-up" by Downsian rules largely because it has come to accept (for a variety of reasons) many of the assumptions which inform such a theory of electoral competition'. With regard to the use of focus groups and opinion polling to reposition the party he roundly declares: 'A more distinctly Downsian strategy could scarcely be imagined'.[3]

The initial principle of public choice theory is quite straightforward: that economic theories of decision-making can be applied to non-market choices. The behaviours and rationalities assumed by utilitarian and individualist models of economic choice are put to use in making sense of those in the public sector. Voting in a legislature, electing an MP, budget demands from public servants and policy decisions by ministers can all be understood by the same models used to explain purchases in a supermarket.[4] It is argued that, despite working in public and non-commercial organisations, state-employed bureaucrats make decisions akin to those of market choice. Bureaucratic actions can be understood as private choices made by individuals. Thus economic theory colonises political science, putting itself forward as rational, scientific and non-normative - the philosopher's stone of positivist social science. Public choice

---

3. See chapter 3 of Colin Hay's *The Political Economy of New Labour*, Manchester University Press 1999.
4. 'When I go to vote I am doing something similar but not identical to what I do when I go shopping. In both cases I "buy" what I "want" ... there are obvious differences between the cases ... but they are similar enough for the public choice analyst to have things worth saying about the citizen's decisions of whether and how to vote, and also about what politicians, bureaucrats and pressure groups do' (Iain McLean, *Public Choice: An Introduction*, Blackwell 1989, pp9-10).

theory argues that all politicians and bureaucrats act in self-interested ways and prides itself on being an accurate depiction of what actually happens in processes of political decision-making rather than a method clouded by collectivist sentimentality.

One result of this is the view that public based systems of provision will inevitably lead to excessive spending. Public Choice Theory applies the logic of microeconomics to politics and generally finds that 'whereas self-interest leads to benign results in the marketplace, it produces nothing but pathology in political decisions'.[5] Because they are not subject to the profit motive and the rigours of competition, there is no limit to what bureaucrats may demand. Similarly, politicians will seek to maximise self-interest by supporting expenditure on programmes that benefit them politically, rather than on programmes that are necessarily effective and fiscally efficient. This point is, naturally, a coded attack on Keynesianism. The conclusion is that the incentive system in public services is all wrong. Actors are encouraged to focus attention on the input side of their organisation (such as finance, staff levels, etc) rather than on the output side (what they actually achieve). The solution is to shift the balance of incentives. In Britain in the 1980s this led to the contracting out of services, the spread of internal markets and outright privatisation. It also led to measurement of outputs through forms of performance assessment and to league tables for schools, hospitals and so on.

This is very damaging for democratic politics because public choice theory treats problems as managerial rather than political. Errors can be rectified through the careful design of managerial systems and structures in ways that bring about the desired change in behaviour. Now, it may well be that because there were minimal constraints in the past, doctors advocated the maximum range of treatments rather than the most efficient ones. It may also be the case that bureaucrats were in a position that encouraged them to act in ways that benefited their organisations more than the people they were supposed to serve. But creating structured incentives is a very particular response to this problem. What it achieves is a guarantee that public servants will act in ways designed to meet the criteria by which they are adjudicated. For example, in universities the introduction of forms of assessment based on published research

---

5. Paul Starr, 'The Meaning of Privatization', *Yale Law and Policy Review*, 6, 1988.

has only served to cause academics to write and publishers to print more. This may have created a further incentive to employ and promote those who publish most (so, perhaps, rewarding the hard-working), and to remove those who were not publishing so much. But the downside is clear. Those with skills in areas not related to publishing (such as teaching) may not be rewarded. The increase in published research is matched by a decrease in attention to teaching. The introduction of performance measurement results in a herd-like rush to fulfil those requirements. Innovation decreases and the volume of published material rises dramatically without any necessary increase in quality. Whatever damaging pursuit of self-interest was hampering the growth of quality in public services has not been eliminated; instead it has been redirected, because acting on self-interest has been re-legitimated not de-legitimated. Academics are encouraged to write not for each other or for a wider public but for their curriculum vitae. The public choice solution to problems across the whole range of public services is to change behaviour via alterations to the environment in which people work. It adjusts the stimuli which act on the organism - the worker or service; it is a system of control and rule rather than a plan for political change. It has nothing to say about what we actually want a public service to do and cannot offer any guidance on this question. Certainly a regime of assessment measures and targeting can change the culture and values of an organisation. But it cannot decide on what we should try to change those values to. That is a political decision related to judgements of a kind quite different to merely individual choice. In entering the public services as a mechanism designed to ensure only efficacy, public choice theory, or the New Public Management, masks the fact that encoded into it are a set of value judgements about the public services. These are removed from the clear purview of political discussion, and shifted onto narrow notions of efficiency. This leads to two factors that further contribute to de-politicisation.

The split between policy and delivery

Firstly, public choice enables government to blame policy failure on the ineptitude of managers who are now kept at arms-length. This was central to the Thatcherite restructuring of the state. If an independent trust hospital fails then government can blame the managers of the trust. If schools fail then responsibility lies with the staff. If prisoners riot then errors must have been

made by prison staff and governors. Decision-making can come to appear to be non-political, merely an 'operational matter'. As Du Gay argues, the split between policy and delivery is 'the ideal organisational innovation for ministers':
... 'ministers still retain formal accountability to Parliament for the conduct of policy and yet are simultaneously able to decide what is and is not a policy issue, they are now in a position to have their cake and eat it'.[6] This process, started by the Tory governments under Thatcher and Major, has been continued by New Labour. Indeed it may have particular advantages for them in that it separates them from total responsibility for public sector wages. Unions have to negotiate with employers rather than with government, so freeing the latter from involvement in damaging industrial relations disputes (though the government have not always been able to successfully maintain this fiction - as was particularly evident in the firefighters' dispute, for example). Of course, this is a strategy that poses problems for government, in that citizens may not be so nuanced in their approach to issues and may continue to regard hospital failure as a proper concern of government. But it is operating in a context in which public services have been undermined politically and organisationally, with the expectations of the public systematically lowered. It thus contributes to a declining sympathy for politics, which it is in the interest of politicians to foster, because it enables them to shift blame for policy failure onto executive agencies, quangos, private contractors and so on (see, for example, Railtrack).

The perverse truth, then, is that all this does actually make sense for those in government in our particular political system. Our form of representative democracy has developed in such a way that, feeling distant from the institutions of state and constituted as an electorate rather than a body of active citizens, people tend to judge the government in terms of their apparent competence as opposed to the actual values which they manifest and attempt to engender in state and society.

This is particularly the case in the field of economic management. Because the ideology and social system that underpins our government is that of capitalism, and it is axiomatic that the state should not really try to interfere in the free actions of economic agents, the government believes it cannot act on this fundamental area of social life. The state, in short, is structurally dependent

---

6. Quoted in John Clarke and Janet Newman, *The Managerial State*, Sage 1997, p144.

upon capital. Thus, as Colin Hay makes plain, New Labour must 'convince capital of the fiscal probity and responsibility of their measures ... while sustaining a popular political project capable of providing a sufficient electoral base'.[7] Given that it has these constraints coming from one side, but is likely to be punished for them from the other, electoral, side, social democratic politics is almost always stuck between Scylla and Charybdis. It thus becomes quite rational for a government to downplay the power it has and to reduce the areas over which it claims political control. Keynesian social-democratic governments fell into crises of legitimation because they could not deliver simultaneously the conditions desired by capital and those promised to labour. Rather than attack capital, such governments vacillated until they fell and were replaced by New Right governments which willingly attacked labour. New Labour has subsequently rejected a politicised engagement with the economy, arguing that it cannot really interfere with it because of the constraints imposed by the globalisation of finance. Instead it prefers to set up rules to which it will adhere in the hope that this will ensure stability of expectations and so confidence in the market, while devolving power to bodies such as the Monetary Policy Committee of the Bank of England. Through this mechanism New Labour can 'seek to evade direct responsibility for high interest rates and the high value of sterling, thus establishing its credibility with the markets whilst, at the same time, increasing the pressure on labour and capital to become more competitive'.[8] The advantage of all this (New Public Management plus a hands-off economic strategy) is that it appears to remove political calculation from the process of economic management. This is deemed an advantage to the markets, but it is also an advantage to the state, in that it cannot be so easily accused of screwing things up since it was only following pre-set rules. Of course, at the same time, it is the government that sets the rules; and what is offered with one, decentralising hand, is taken away by the other, which intensifies systems of regulation and rule-setting, allowing government to pretend that it is on the side of the citizen and is bashing those nasty professionals in their name. Depoliticisation is thus a highly political strategy, with the effect of shifting regimes

---

7. See Chapter 5 of Colin Hay's book.
8. Peter Burnham, 'New Labour and the politics of depoliticisation', *British Journal of Politics and International Relations*, Vol. 3, No. 2, 2001, p139.

of accountability and influence away from the elected and thus away from the electors. This has even wider effects on 'political culture'. This brings us to the second way in which public choice and attendant ideologies contribute to a general depoliticisation.

The individualisation of public activity

Public choice theory adds to, and extends, the individualisation of all public activity. Far from combating individualism, the ideology of new public management entrenches it, reinforcing the values of market individualism rather than bolstering those of public service. It facilitates (and one cannot help but suspect this was the purpose) the spread of values of individualism and the virtues of market mechanisms of allocation over all others. This happens at the level of the manager but also at that of the user of a public service. The introduction of managerialism into the public services is also a process 'through which new subject positions are created, through which "administrators", "public servants" and "practitioners" come to see themselves as "business managers", "purchasers", "contractors", "strategists", "leaders" and so on'.[9] Workers in public services are encouraged to see themselves as entrepreneurs and 'change agents', as individual actors rather than parts of collective enterprises. Indeed, this is understood as a positive form of liberation, moving away from hierarchical and protective forms of activity to empowering and open networks. To be sure, this may well have the effect of undermining certain monopolies of power, and damaging forms of prejudicial and defensive inertia, but the cost is that of further breaking public services away from their public positioning, undermining their collective commitment and replacing it with a looser sense of public good based on satisfying customer need. Thus, the individualisation goes all the way through the services and starts to reconfigure the user and the user experience. Here, the New Public Management and public choice theory combine with more general management theory, which advocates a focus on attracting and holding onto customers through the provision of an all-round quality consumption experience. This may encourage service managers to see the people they serve as diverse and differentiated and as something other than a homogeneous mass requiring and deserving exactly the same things. As such the move towards a

---

9. *The Managerial State*, p92.

customer oriented rhetoric is not simply a product of the New Right obsession with efficiency; it also accords with New Left critiques of the bureaucratic nature of state services, and the defensive and restrictive power of organised professionals. However:

> Consumerism can help authorities to advance from considering individual members of the public as passive clients or recipients of services ... but it will rarely be enough to turn members of the public into partners actively involved in shaping public services ... it does not go far enough to effect a radical shift in the distribution of power.[10]

Our immediate interest here is not in how this discourse of consumerism affects public services, but in its wider impact on understandings of the political. Here Clarke and Newman are incisive when they comment on the Thatcherite reforms of the state, and their development of market relations in public services: 'These changes aimed to dislocate collectivist notions of the public and the public interest, challenging the legitimacy of any claims (other than those of national government) to be able to speak for the people' (p123).

This, then, is the background against which New Labour's commitment to the 'democratising of democracy' must be placed. On the one hand there are genuine shifts in the ways in which people perceive themselves and their aspirations, as well as their expectations of what politics can do. People are more aware of their variations and distinct needs, and we do now live in societies made up of people with more diverse lifestyles and backgrounds. It is harder for the media to function as a meaningful public space (and they are not much inclined to do so), and nations and national states appear to be less significant determinants of social life. But these shifts are inseparable from the wider context of democratic practice in liberal capitalist societies, in which certain centres of power - those rooted in economic activity - are not to be challenged by government, and where the primary form of political power that can be exercised by the citizen is the vote or party membership. Political decisions lie behind the deregulation of media, and their insertion into market logics that militate against their playing a more considered public and democratically accountable role.

---

10. J. Potter, quoted in *The Managerial State*, pp108-9.

The extension of public choice and of market mechanisms throughout the public services has been a matter of political will, and it has spread and secured an ideology that is hostile to collective action, and ensured that political problems are mostly seen as attributable to management failure. As Hobsbawm succinctly puts it:

> Market sovereignty ... is an alternative to any kind of politics, as it denies the need for *political* decisions, which are precisely decisions about common or group interests as distinct from the sum of choices, rational or otherwise, of individuals pursuing private preferences. Participation in the market replaces participation in politics. The consumer takes the place of the citizen.[11]

Politics thus comes to lose all appeal. It seems an unwieldy way of making decisions that are essentially to do with my personal preferences rather than with any attempt I may make to see things from a collective or public point of view. The management of personal life just as much as the management of industry or social services becomes a matter of calculating what is most efficient, what has minimum opportunity cost, what will be most immediately profitable.

The need for democracy

This anti-political aspect of New Labour is particularly damaging for its stated aim of reforming public services, which cannot be achieved through the fixing of incentive structures. In an important piece of work, Peter Taylor-Gooby conducted survey research into the attitudes of the public sector salariat, to establish why they sometimes seem 'conservative' in the face of government initiated reforms. Public choice theory might suggest that the reason for inertia is that the cosy interests of such workers are being threatened. But Taylor-Gooby shows that these are not conservative, idle, self-interested and inert people. Quite simply they have an intellectual difference of opinion with the government.[12] They do not regard the problems of welfare claimants as their individual failure, but endorse the 'traditional' view that welfare polices should be directed towards structural or systemic disadvantage. To put it simply, the

---

11. Eric Hobsbawm, 'Democracy can be Bad for You', *New Statesman*, 5.3.01.
12. Peter Taylor-Gooby, 'Blair's Scars', *Critical Social Policy*, 64, 20: 3, 2000, pp331-348.

government has not won the argument with them. If the government wants to transform public services it needs to do so not only through instituting certain systems of management, but by campaigning for its programme. But winning people over politically means forging a coalition with them. It also means making use of one of the key benefits of democracy. If people feel they have participated fairly in the shaping and taking of a decision they are more likely to pursue and act on it even if it was not their original first choice. Just as we accept governments we do not support, because we feel we played a part in their selection and were fairly defeated, so people who work in large organisations (state or private) will work better for them if they feel they have some power or control over what it is they are doing. If they experience change as something imposed on them from above (and so cannot see the reasons for it or feel 'ownership' over it), they may comply but will not endorse and, as every management theorist knows, compliance is not enough. One needs the employee to feel committed to the project of the enterprise.

This highlights a key problem for much current management theory, at least the variety which permeates government circles and the public sector: the talk is all about freeing up the worker, giving them control over their skills and labour, allowing them to be creative and so forth - all sounding very democratic and emancipatory. But such liberty does not necessarily imply democracy: they are not the same thing. Such theory does not acknowledge that democracy requires participation in collective discussion about goals; it is not simply a question of being free as an individual to respond to a fixed number of individual choices.

While you cannot have democracy without liberty, you can have liberty without democracy. It is quite possible formally to be free, to do as you please as far as able, without being attached to a social group in which decisions are made collectively and openly. This is the ideal state for the libertarian ideology, but that is quite different to democracy. The ideal of democracy (as opposed to that of pure liberty) is that one is attached to a social group (a collective of some kind) within which decisions are taken (collectively and openly) as to the ordering of relations within that group. While this entails certain restrictions on the absolute liberty of each individual, it also means that they are better placed to take some control over the sorts of choices that are put before them. The libertarian individual can only respond with freedom to that which is put before them. He or she is still constrained by the structure of the society in which he or she lives. The democratic individual is able to have some say over that structure. This is why (as every true liberal knows and as John Stuart Mill made plain) democracy is to be understood as a transformatory system: it changes the individuals who participate in it and they in turn change the kind of society in which they live. Thus, when liberty and democracy are conjoined they produce great benefits. We are free to make and act on decisions, but that freedom is usefully constrained by our participation in a wider social group. We can escape that group if we find it stifling, but we might well find it to be a useful way in which to advance our liberty and our understanding of ourselves. Furthermore, we do not have all the answers to all the problems we face, and we need to be in a position to have our ideas, our preferences, shaped and re-shaped in the encounter, in the dialogue, with others. In the Kantian ideal we exercise our public reason, which is not only reasoning in or by a public, but also an attempt to think at the public level, to think about what is best for all as well as for ourselves. The narrow horizons of public choice theory cannot encompass this.

In spite of the rhetoric, taking away the old bureaucratic systems of power is not the same as giving power. But this is what people need, especially in public services: power to come to decisions, in concert, about how to organise things. New Labour appears at times to want to give workers in public services a bit of room to 'innovate', but this is usually within narrow parameters. Incentives and charter marks may help, a little, in the breaking down of bureaucracy. But history teaches us that the only way to really break away from stultifying absolutism and centralisation is to have a democratic revolution, and let power go the subjects of rule.

Within society generally there is a pluralisation of politics underway (indeed in this sphere, the depoliticisation thesis has little purchase). This is not simply a pluralisation of the different views or positions people hold and take, but of the sites and forms of political activity. Much attention is paid to the 'new social movements', but there are also many lower level and local campaigns, often involving developments in schools, hospitals, in streets and parks and, crucially, in the workplace. If democracy is to spread and deepen, it will do so not simply in the form of increased liberty (the removal of power), but in the form of increased capacity to take control of different spheres of our lives (the increase and spread of power). Democracy emerged as opposition to absolutist forms of rule. It was thus often conceived in terms of limiting the power of authorities to interfere in the lives of citizens. But as the democratic revolution spread and developed, it became clear that the absence of restraint was not enough. Democratic practice came not only to define the relationship of state to citizen, but also of citizens to each other, of citizens to themselves and of citizens to their world. Consequently it meant the getting and using of power and not just its evasion.

The spheres of state, individual, society and economy have become ever more complex, blurred and inter-related. But this makes politics more important not less. Pick your metaphor, but politics is the glue that binds them, the oil that keeps their relationship smooth. When contradictions arise (as they often do) between the different dimensions of our lives (as citizens, as private people, as social beings, as workers), it is politics that can articulate them and establish a new way of ordering. Politics needs to be understood as the sphere of life where we decide on how to order these relationships and set goals for ourselves, and this can only be done in concert with others.

And here the democratisation of work is crucial. As we spend more of our time in work, and as systems of management become more extensive or all encompassing, then we need to have some sort of reconfigured relationship between worker and corporation. It is now not enough simply to have legal protections for workers, procedures by which grievances and disputes are resolved. It is also vital to have political systems that open up and democratise the workplace. Such would be an important step towards putting the economy back in touch with the world from whence it came and making a reality of that which certain management theories pretend to be the case.

But we should also keep hold of the vision of a society that fulfils the promise of our technology and our fantastic productive capacity. There is a rich heritage in left-wing thinking that can fill out such a vision with a commitment to freeing societies from the despotism of the economic, and the reduction of everything to the price it reaches at market. New forms of technology very probably do possess the capacity to improve aspects of the lives of many millions. But they will not do so of themselves, since technologies possess no capacity for self-direction. The political question concerns how we are to envisage these new forms of social and economic potential. What is to be the focus that guides their implementation, so that we can benefit from their capacity to liberate us from old forms of futile desire and helpless drudgery, and from the necessity that we attune ourselves to the economy as the price of inclusion? The blurring of blue collar and white collar work, seen by some as evidence of the democratising effects of new modes of labour, can easily be achieved by pushing everyone down rather than lifting everyone up.

Momentous transformations cannot be ignored or refused, but they should be treated as transformations that we are bringing about, whose direction will derive from the decisions we take. This is also why democratisation cannot be equated with marketisation. We need to be empowered not simply to say yes or no, buy or sell, but to question the terms of debates, invent new choices and feel they belong to us.

This article is an extract from Alan Finlayson's Making Sense of New Labour, *published by Lawrence & Wishart in 2003. To order a copy postfree, email orders@lwbooks.co.uk or call 020 8533 2506.*

Making Sense of New Labour

Alan Finlayson

An in-depth study of New Labour, interpreting a wide range of material, including party political broadcasts, Tony Blair's speeches, and internal policy discussion. Finlayson argues that New Labour's political philosophy is in large part a reflection of the culture and politics of contemporary capitalism, which means that it inevitably finds itself managing a status quo rather than driving genuine change.

' Alan Finlayson brings off an invaluable analysis of the framing assumptions of the New Labour project. This is a book which both critics and supporters of New Labour need to read. '

Michael Rustin

£16.99 Available post-free from Lawrence & Wishart,
99a Wallis Rd, London, E9 5LN
Tel: 020 8533 2506 E-mail:orders@lwbooks.co.uk

PFI: The only show in town

Jonathan Rutherford

Jonathan Rutherford looks at the policies and infrastructure that have been put into place in order to create a new area of market activity.

The ideological dynamo driving New Labour is the transformation of the public sector. Peter Mandelson set out the task at the Progressive Governance Conference in July 2002, 'We [must] challenge the status quo and fundamentally redesign monolithic, largely state provided and centrally managed public services'.[1] As Tony Blair describes it: 'We should be far more radical about the role of the state as a regulator rather than a provider ... We should also stimulate new entrants to the schools market, and be willing to experiment with new forms of co-payment in the public sector'.[2] New Labour modernisation is giving shape to a new kind of liberal or market state, designed to promote economic efficiency and individual choice. Central to this development is the private financing of public capital spending.

New Labour's rhetoric conjures up an image of an overweening state squandering a huge proportion of GDP on 'one-size-fits-all, take-it-or-leave-it public services'. But historically the UK has had relatively low levels of public spending compared to other European countries. Public sector net investment as a percentage of GDP rose to an all time high of 7.5 per cent in 1968-69, but then it fell precipitously. By 1988-89 it was 0.5 per cent. It rose to 2.1 per cent in 1992-93, before sinking back to 0.4

---

1. Peter Mandelson, 'Editorial', *Progressive Politics*, Vol. 2.1, January 2003, p4.
2. Tony Blair, 'Progressive Governance', *Progressive Politics*, p9.

per cent in 1998.[3] When New Labour took office in 1997, it inherited over three decades of chronic under-investment in public assets and infrastructure, and a £27bn deficit. For its first two years, it maintained the spending plans of the previous Conservative administration, thus presiding over further cuts in capital spending of 4.7 per cent a year. In the final three years of its first term, it then increased capital spending by 24.8 per cent over the period, but this made only a small impact on the downward trend. The fruit of New Labour's historic landslide election was a level of capital spending still considerably less than that during the brief Tory boom of 1992-93.

In 1994, John Prescott and Gordon Brown published *Financing Infrastructure Investment - Promoting a Partnership Between Public and Private Finance*, a document which set out New Labour's approach to public sector investment. They described it as an alternative to the Conservative policy of privatisation. Their claim was rather disingenuous. By 1993 the UK programme of privatisation had already peaked; the supply of politically acceptable, saleable state assets was all but exhausted. New Labour's Public Private Partnerships were thus not so much an alternative to privatisation, they were more an opportunity to further develop the liberalisation of the state and public sector, by other means. Using the private sector to design, build, finance and operate (DBFO) public assets and infrastructure would open up new markets, particularly in education and health, in areas which had previously been off-limits to private sector involvement. The chosen instrument for New Labour's market-based modernisation was the Private Finance Initiative (PFI). Private capital would support and resource public services for public need. Its pursuit of optimal returns on its investment would drive down costs, introduce new ways of working, and promote innovation and efficiency. The market would also encourage greater local control of service provision.

The PFI had been launched in 1992 by Conservative Chancellor Norman Lamont. It had been intended as an accounting device to limit public borrowing and keep capital investment off the public sector balance sheet, but had suffered a rather lacklustre performance. New Labour pledged to reinvigorate it. In 1997, Malcolm Bates, chairman of Pearl Assurance, undertook a review. Paymaster

---

3. Institute of Fiscal Studies, 'Issues in Public Spending', *The IFS Green Budget 2000*, p36, www.ifs.org.uk.

General Geoffrey Robinson and his advisors from consultants Arthur Anderson then turned his recommendations into a new Treasury PFI Task Force. The Tories' idea of outsourcing public sector infrastructure was extended as a means to create an alternative income stream for financing public services. A second Bates review transformed the Taskforce into Partnerships UK (PUK). Based inside the Treasury, PUK was launched in June 2000, with a 51 per cent stake sold to 'qualifying' private sector institutions. Treasury Minister Andrew Smith announced: 'By turning Partnerships UK into a public private partnership the Government is creating a key market opening for private sector shareholders, keen to seize the opportunity to help the public sector deliver modern, high quality public services'.[4]

With a remit to promote PFI both at home and overseas, the success of PUK depended upon encouraging private sector interest. Stephen Timms, Financial Secretary to the Treasury, told the Private Finance Initiative Global Summit in Cape Town in 2000: 'I am delighted to be able to announce today that Partnerships UK is to provide strategic support for the development of public private partnerships in South Africa … This is the first international agreement of its kind'.[5] Back in the UK, in November 2000 Gordon Brown told the Private Finance Annual Conference: 'I hope bankers and their credit committees get the sense of security they intuitively search for … in the very real continuous flow of business opportunities that schools, hospitals, prisons, roads and government accommodation projects offer for the long term. These are core services which Government, whether local or central, is statutorily duty-bound to provide, and for which demand is virtually insatiable … Where else can you get a long term business opportunity like that.'[6]

The Private Finance Initiative

PFI projects are designed to fund long-term infrastructure and public services. Debt (funds raised by bank loan or on the market) and equity (shares) used to finance the project are paid back from the revenues it

---

4. 'New Business Opportunities to Create Public Private Partnerships - Andrew Smith', Treasury Press Release, 19 December 2001, www.hmtreasury.gov.uk.
5. Keynote speech by Stephen Timms MP at PFI Global Summit, Cape Town, SA, 6.12.00, www.privatefinance-i.com.
6. Chancellor's speech to the 2000 Private Finance Annual Conference, www.privatefinance-i.com.

generates. A typical PFI scheme involves the public sector client, the private sector operator, the financial lender, the building contractor and sub contractors, a number of technical, financial and legal advisers, and the facilities management team. The private sector establishes an independent legal company called the Special Purpose Vehicle. The shareholders of the operator invest equity in the SPV, and the lender - a financial institution - funds the remainder of the cost. The SPV allows the operator and contractor to keep debt off their balance sheets, and so protect their equity in the event of failure. This separate company bids for the PFI contract, which details the services to be provided and the conditions for their delivery. It defines the parties with a legitimate interest in decisions affecting the project and its outcomes only as those contractually involved. What pertains to be relevant to the scheme is what is written in the contract.

The PFI contract has an important effect. It shifts the proposed service and its delivery out of the public discourse of democratic decision-making and into the realm of commercial law. It serves to disentangle the service provision from its social ties. Michel Callon argues that for an object to become a commodity it must become an object of calculability, and must be 'disentangled' from its social ties so that it can be sold. The market must frame its actors and their relations in order to make them clearly distinct and disassociated from one another.[7] Alternatively, these social entanglements need to be 'internalised' and brought within the frame of market calculation. The PFI contract creates both a market regime and an enlarged space of calculability. The effect is to disaggregate public sector services and reintegrate them into new markets as a series of commodities. In these markets the frontier between the public and private sectors, and between social and economic domains, is being redefined. The social values of public service are displaced by consumer choice and cost benefit analysis. F.A. Hayek makes the broader point in his 'The Principle of a Liberal Social Order': 'Strictly speaking it is meaningless to speak of a value "to society" when what is in question is the value of some services to certain people, services which may be of no interest to anybody else'.[8]

---

7. See, for example, Michel Callon, 'Keynote Speech: Actor-Network Theory - The Market Test', July 1997, www.comp.lancs.ac.uk/sociology/stscallon1.html.
8. F.A. Hayek, *Studies in Philosophy, Politics and Economics*, Routledge and Kegan Paul 1978, p172.

The PFI contract

The case for PFI has been justified on the basis of a division between non-core, infrastructural services and core social-domain services like teaching and medical care. But such a division has already been substantially broken down across the public sector, through a range of techniques - such as Public Service Agreements, performance-based public management systems, regimes of best practice and Value for Money. VfM institutionalises comparisons with the private sector through its focus on targets, competitions and cost. Its effect is to introduce economic calculation into what were previously social and bureaucratic domains, making them receptive to private sector participation. Furthermore, there is evidence that the aspiration of private companies to manage and deliver core services is shared by government. For example, new DfES guidelines on PFI have the effect of speeding up 'the transformation of the school estate', using criteria which are based on 'proving that the project will help transform educational attainment'. This is an invitation for private companies to cross the divide into service provision. The Department recently awarded Jarvis Educational Services Ltd, the education arm of engineering company Jarvis, a £1.9m three-year contract to intervene in failing schools. Nick Blackwell, chief executive of Jarvis Educational Services Ltd, did however argue that he would employ a mixture of businessmen and educationists: 'Our role is not to interfere in schools or LEAs', he assured the sceptics. 'Our role is to help with capacity and support for these programmes. We don't go anywhere near teaching staff or the classroom'.[9] But whatever happens with this particular contract, it is part of an attempt to widen the scope for private sector involvement across the board.

Actors in the PFI market

The financial services industry is the driving force behind the developing PFI market. In the early days of PFI, investors were primarily contractors and a few banks, such as Barclays European Infrastructure Fund and Innisfree. As the market has matured, banks have been taking up new, more central, roles, as financial advisers, equity investors, senior lenders and - a relatively recent development - bond issuers. Financial investors now include pension funds, specialist infrastructure funds and insurance companies. The influence of the

---

9. 'School contract for rail crash inquiry firm', *Guardian*, 28.4.03.

City is reflected in the number of institutions which have an equity stake in Partnerships UK. Abbey National Treasury Services plc, Sun Life Assurance plc, The Prudential Assurance Company Ltd, Barclays Industrial Investments Ltd, The Royal Bank of Scotland plc/Bank of Scotland and Halifax Projects Investments Ltd, together form the great majority of Partnerships UK shareholders. Amongst the current Board of Directors there is a preponderance of banking interests.

'equity return on Balfour Beatty's PFI projects is expected to be between 13 and 18 percent'

A growing number of financial institutions have established longer term strategic partnerships with construction companies, for example with Accord, Alfred McAlpine, AMEC, Balfour Beatty, Bovis, Jarvis, John Laing and Kier Project Investment Ltd. The PFI is transforming the construction and engineering sector, as companies turn themselves into Support Services' Infrastructure Management Companies. Thus leading arms manufacturer Vosper Thorneycroft set up VT Education, an £80m a year business which owns the Careers Management Group, who provide Connexion services in areas of London and the South. VT has recently acquired the supplier of schools inspection services, Westminster Education Consultants Ltd. In May 2003, it agreed a £100m, seven-year deal with Surrey county council to run a joint company aiming to win contracts from failing LEAs. The change from traditional engineering or construction to service and asset management is proving profitable. In March 2002, Balfour Beatty announced profits up by 20 per cent. Its traditional civil engineering business produced profit margins of between 3 per cent and 4 per cent. Equity return on investment in its 11 PFI projects was expected to be between 13 per cent and 17 per cent or 18 per cent.

The increasing number of small and first-time PFI schemes being promoted by inexperienced public sector organisations has meant a greater reliance on professional advisers for this sector. The large accountancy corporations are ubiquitous, advising both private and public sector clients. PriceWaterhouseCoopers is the leading PFI adviser, with a large practice of 170 PFI projects across the UK. It is also auditor to 22 local authorities. Despite this interest, Tony Blair cited its 2001 report, *Public Private Partnerships: A Clearer View*, as providing 'overwhelming evidence' that PFI was 'excellent value for money'.[10] Another accounting firm, KPMG, has negotiated more than £22.2bn of public sector deals using PFI and PPP, and provides audit services to over 40 per cent of Higher Education Institutions in the UK, and over 30 per cent of FE Colleges. Apart from standard non-core services, a team of KPMG advisors will, as part of its contractual duties, be reviewing funding, curriculum re-engineering, responses to curriculum 2000, and the development of information learning and teaching strategies. Law firms are also significant actors in the PFI market. In 2001, Clifford Chance was voted the top PFI law firm on the PFI portal PrivateFinance-i.com. The winner in the education sector was Eversheds, with over 94 HEIs and 230 FE colleges. John Boardman, head of Eversheds' Education North, commenting on its recent contract with Sheffield Hallam University, identified the source of law firms' expanding work in the sector: 'The appointment highlights an increasing drive within the education sector for universities to put more of their services out to tender'.[11] In 2000, Eversheds held its round Britain 'Trade Union Roadshow', informing employers about its trade-union-resistance practice.

Projects in the more established PFI sectors - such as prisons, hospitals and DBFO roads - are drawing together these different agencies in order to replicate the documentation, finance agreements, and payment mechanisms of earlier PFI transactions. The aim is to standardise procedures, cut the procurement period and lower the high costs of bidding for contracts. The demand for standardisation and economies of scale is encouraging the 'bundling' of schemes across services such as housing, schools, social services into single larger packages. This arrangement makes subsequent contracts easier and cheaper to secure, and further integrates public-sector provision into the market. Partnerships are becoming self-standing companies, using existing revenue-generating PFIs to bid for new schemes. In turn, government policy, particularly its Comprehensive Spending Reviews, is driving public bodies down the PFI route. The result is a trend toward a corporate welfare network, in which the high bidding costs favour large established corporations. In May 2002 the Government formalised this corporate welfare approach with the institution

---

10. Parliamentary answer in response to a question from Annabelle Ewing MP, House of Commons. See www.gmb.org.uk/docs/pdfs/pricewater.pdf.
11. Press Release, www.eversheds.com/about/newsandcomment.asp.

of a series of Joint Service Centres in five authorities. The PFI scheme in Manchester will build a centre providing a library, employment and advice services, adult education, family and primary healthcare.

Capital markets

Less obviously, but no less significantly, the PFI is integrating public services into the capital markets. The costs of financing PFI projects are being driven down by increasingly sophisticated multi-product approaches. Historically, debt-funding for PFI has come from banks. But more recently bond issues are being used as a major source of long-term project finance. The current programme of NHS PFI schemes will largely be funded in the bond market. By March 2002, £700m of bond debt had been raised for these projects. Because corporate bonds carry a higher risk than government bonds, they are valued by international rating agencies. To secure a good rating and lower the cost of long-term funding, companies take out insurance on the bonds they issue. Businesses that provide this kind of insurance are called Monolines (because it is the only type of insurance they offer). They guarantee to make timely payment of principal and interest if the bond issuer fails to do so. Monoline insurance is particularly important for SPVs, because their bonds are rated on the weakest of the parties with material obligations in the PFI project.

Monoline insurers are now significant actors in the PFI market. In the UK, the US-owned AMBAC UK and MBIA both guaranteed a £30m bond issue by the Royal Bank of Canada Financial Group, for the Greenwich University PFI. A third US Monoline, Financial Security Assurance Inc (FSA), was bought in 2000 by leading European Bank Dexia, for $2.6bn. Dexia has acted as arranger and lender in more than 20 UK PFI projects. Pierre Richard, CEO of the Management Board of Dexia, told a June 2002 meeting in Paris: 'For the Dexia Group as a whole, public sector clients are a mine ... we are just beginning to exploit them'.[12]

In Higher Education, the new income stream created by student fees is likely to entangle university funding in the capital markets. Banks are beginning to play an increasing role in buying and selling student debt, and funding university growth and development through public private partnerships and debt finance.

---

12. Press Release, 21.6.02, www.Dexia.com/uk/news/pressreleases.

Standard & Poor's Ratings Services report *Higher Education: Changing by Degrees* (March 2003) was one signal of the growing interest of the financial services industry. The involvement of capital markets in funding Higher Education will expose universities to potentially damaging levels of risk, and intensify the dynamics of inequality in the sector. Keele University, in an attempt to overcome its chronic underfunding, leased its halls of residence to a specially created company Owengate Keele plc. As well as receiving a twenty-five-year income stream from student rent, Owengate would raise funds on the bond market to pay the university a cash premium of £65m. The deal failed to deliver the full £65m, and the loss of rent deprived the university of income for paying staff wages; what is more, bond repayment takes precedent over all other budget items, including student rents and staff salaries. The longer-term consequences of the scheme threaten serious financial problems.[13] Last year, the University of Hertfordshire agreed a £190m PFI deal with Carillion for accommodation for 1600 students and extensive sports facilities. Funding for the project is by a £60 million Limited Price Index (LPI) bond issue, wrapped by Monoline FSA. LPI bonds reduce the risk to the private sector by capping payment liabilities at between 0 per cent and 5 per cent. Increases above 5 per cent and decreases below 0 per cent must be met by the university. Again, bond repayments will take precedence over rents and staff costs. The deal exposes the university to potentially high levels of risk.[14]

To be effective financial instruments, bonds require a secondary market. In primary financial markets companies raise capital, and money flows from lenders to borrowers. In secondary markets investors buy and sell existing assets amongst themselves. An active secondary market persuades investors to take on new assets in the primary market, knowing that they can sell them if they need to. In 2002 PFI projects became established in the secondary market. M&G and Innisfree launched a £100m PFI fund. Abbey National and Babcock and Brown set up the Secondary Market and Infrastructure and Facilities Fund, managing £1.5bn worth of PFI and PPP assets. In the same month, Monoline Ambac UK initiated a European insurance programme which would allow investors in project finance to transfer bond and

---

13. 'Owengate', *Guardian Education*, 27.5.03.
14. 'The perfect hedge or a perfect storm', *Project Finance International*, Issue 236, 6.3.02.

insurance policies in the secondary market. Increasing the liquidity of PFI bond financing encourages the global buying and selling, and hence ownership of, PFI project debt. It is the guaranteed long-term income stream that makes PFI an attractive asset to the capital markets. Once a PFI project has completed the development phase, the cash flow begins and its risk profile is reduced. The private-sector partners will seek to refinance the project by lowering the amount of equity in the project and replacing the original bank debt with new bank debt at lower interest rates. For example, Group 4 and Carillion were able to greatly increase their profits on Fazakerly (now Altcourse) prison. The majority of the 75 per cent increase in profits they achieved - £10.7m of it - came from extending the bank loan period at a reduced interest rate, and early repayment of debt. In response the Office of Government Commerce issued a voluntary code of conduct, 'to enable private sector contractors to share refinancing gain with the public sector.'[15] However, the code is unlikely to stop companies seeking to maximise their gains through rearranging debt and equity finance.

Market failures

It would be mistaken to think that constructing PFI markets has been straightforward. There have been a number of spectacular market failures, which has encouraged a wariness in institutional investors. One example of market failure was the consultancy and facilities management group WS Atkins, which joined with Innisfree PFI Fund, and construction and support services group John Mowlem and Company plc, to form NewSchools. The consortium has a £200m, 25-year contract to upgrade the schools of Cornwall, as well as projects in the London Boroughs of Waltham Forest and Merton. WS Atkins also had a £150m, five-year deal with the London Borough of Southwark to run its schools. In July 2002 WS Atkins's share price began to fall. In November it disbanded its education outsource department, resulting in the sacking of 400 employees and its Head of Education.

Amey and Nord Anglia won the £200m school improvement contract in the London Borough of Waltham Forest. The partnership also runs the Abbeylands School in Guildford, Surrey, the first state-school in the UK to be

---

15. Refinancing of Early PFI Transactions Code of Conduct. See also OGC Guidance Note on Calculation of the Authority's Share of a Refinancing Gain, www.pfi.ogc.gov.uk.

run by the private sector. In addition Amey had the Glasgow Schools PPP contract, worth £1.2bn, and the Edinburgh Schools PFI at £360m, and it held a major stake in the Unity City Academy in Middlesbrough. David McGahey, MD of Amey Education, in his presentation 'Vision for Amey Education by 2004', stated that their aim was to be 'lead private sector player/partner in the drive to raise standards and improve effectiveness throughout the UK Education Service'.[16] In March 2002 Amey unveiled losses of £18m after introducing a new system of accounting. The City had been expecting it to announce pre-tax profits of £53m. Market reaction was swift and merciless. Share prices in Amey collapsed, and its finance director left, followed five weeks later by his successor, followed by its chief executive. Its future existence uncertain, Amey has sold all its stakes in PFI contracts.

The market will punish failing PFI companies. Equally, it will expose profitable PFIs to take-over. In 2000, Edison Capital, a subsidiary of US electricity company Edison International, entered a joint venture with Scottish contractor Morrison Construction to take control of 5 PFI schemes. It was the first example of 'bundling' PFI projects, and one of the steps towards the creation of a secondary PFI market. Then in September 2000 Morrison was acquired by the Anglian Water Group as it branched out into infrastructure management. But when AWG lawyers discovered unexpected losses at Morrison, AWG pre-tax profits fell by 38 per cent, creating problems for the planned securitisation of its assets. The ongoing rancour between Morrison and AWG resulted in High Court Action, with the latter claiming £130m damages. Subsequently, in June 2001 Noble PFI Fund acquired Edison Capital's UK PFI investment portfolio, thus securing ten PFI hospital projects and a 50:50 joint venture with Morrison Construction. The complexity of this emerging secondary market raises questions about the ownership of, and policy towards, PFI projects.

A new market state?

By April 2003 the Office of Government Commerce reported a total of 570 signed PFI projects, at a capital value of £352bn. The PFI is thus still a small percentage of total government spending, and as the Institute for Fiscal Studies argues: 'its current impact on the historically low levels of public investment is

---

16. www.amey.co.uk/assets/asset.

minimal.'[17] Nevertheless, in the context of the widespread use of outsourcing, and the market-based changes in public sector organisation, it is part of a significant ideological transformation of the state. But is the PFI simply an expensive distraction from the overwhelming need for massive, cost-effective public investment? The claim that the PFI achieves efficiency gains, and improves service provision through market competition does not stand up on the available evidence.

Government represents the cost of a PFI scheme by its capital value. This is based on public sector estimates for capital expenditure, which are, on average, just 22% of actual costs. When a new PFI is proposed, a decision whether or not to proceed with it is determined by its Value for Money. The Value for Money of each PFI is calculated as its Net Present Value (NPV). The NPV is the cost of the project for each year of the contract, discounted to what the project would be worth at today's prices. Discounting allows for the depreciation in the value of money over time.

This method is biased, because it gives long-term PFI projects a lower NPV than traditional projects, where costs must be met over a few years. It also obscures the issue of their affordability. For example, the Liverpool Grouped Schools scheme has a capital value of £372.5m. The project was signed by Jarvis, who claim in their 2002 interim results that the scheme will earn them £3257m. The extension to Wythenshawe Hospital in South Manchester is put in at £365.6m. Alfred McAlpine, the contractor, reports total revenue flows will be £3550m over thirty-five years, plus additional equity returns through renegotiating its loans after completion. Its 2002 annual report cites seven investments in PFI schemes, with £325.3m of capital committed, for lifetime revenues of £3878m.

Value for Money is treated as an objective calculation, but it is not. The Value for Money of PFI schemes is worked out using a Public Sector Comparator (PSC). The PSC is designed to compare the cost of a private sector bid with the cost of doing the project within the public sector. The problem is that there is no actually existing public sector comparison for bids for large scale or bundled projects. Local authorities, knowing it's the only

---

17. *Twenty-Five Years of Falling Investment? Trends in Capital Spending on Public Services*, Briefing Note No.20, The Institute of Fiscal Studies, www.ifs.org.uk.

show in town, and with the connivance of government officials, have an interest in ensuring that the PSC is calculated to produce an outline business plan that is higher than the private sector bid: no PFI, no new school. Take into account this political chicanery, eliminate from the calculation the high cost of private borrowing compared to public borrowing, by defining it as a private sector risk, add in advantageous land sales and asset transfers, quietly bend a building regulation or two, ignore the fact that central government repayments for the scheme do not coincide with its lifespan, and the public sector often bears considerably greater costs than implied by a scheme's official NPV. Attempts to work out the true financial implications of a PFI are confounded by the obfuscating arts of corporate accountancy, and the sheer complexity of the contract and project financing.

Broader figures give some indication of the longer term costs of the PFI. In 1997-98, the private sector invested £31.5bn in the PFI, and in 1998-99 it invested £32.2bn, guaranteeing repayments until 2026-27. In the years of optimum returns between 2003-04 and 2012-13, these repayments will be worth over £33.5bn a year.[18] Future generations are committed to these levels of capital costs repayments and have been pre-allocated current spending over which they have no control. There might be some justification for this poor commercial practice if the private sector really were guaranteed to be more cost-effective than the public sector in providing its services and in handling risk. But no such guarantee exists. Future repayments are ring-fenced, with a majority of PFI schemes having no mechanism for ensuring value for money over the project's lifetime. Furthermore, if, for example, a school's funding is cut, its PFI repayment takes priority over all other items in the school's budget. The public sector and the tax-payer are locked into contracts that will be very expensive to end. The Public Accounts Committee Report on PFI stated that: 'We are very concerned that over one in five authorities consider that value for money from their PFI contracts has diminished.'[19] The Institute for Fiscal Studies has stated: 'In the absence of continued efficiency improvements in the private sector, any PFI project will now be offering less good value for money than

---

18. *IFS Green Budget 2000*, p36.
19. The Public Accounts Committee 42nd Report, 'Managing the relationship to secure a successful partnership in PFI projects', July 2002, www.parliament.uk/commons/selcom/pachome.htm.

previously was the case.'[20]

On a global level, the influential European Services Forum is lobbying for public procurement in services to be part of the GATS, a move which will increase the liberalisation of the secondary market in PFIs.[21] There are important questions to be asked about the growing encroachment of capital markets into public service provision, about who owns and is accountable for PFI schemes, and about their affordability in the long term. The government has actively promoted PFIs in education at a time when the DfES has reported year on year massive underspends in its budget; and the Treasury's current account surplus for 2000-01 alone was £323bn. Aside from the questions of accountability and budgeting, perhaps a more significant question is what alternatives can be offered by social democratic critiques of PFI and the market state. In a speech promoting the 'partnership approach', Deputy Prime Minister John Prescott said, 'I am well aware that there is a good deal of controversy about bringing private funding into public services. But I am also well aware that politics is the art of the possible.'[22] In many respects New Labour, with its commitment to market-based reform of the public sector, has presided over the diminishing of its own political possibilities. Peter Hain's recent attempt to break this impasse and kick-start a debate about taxation raises questions for critics of the PFI: where would we draw the line on the economic activity of the market? How might we make the public sector an effective provider of social security and an equitable distributor of life chances? These questions need to be addressed both ideologically and pragmatically - not through some pie in the sky scheme for a distant, ever-receding future, but as practical alternatives, underpinned by social democratic priorities.

---

20. IFS Green Budget 2000, p38.
21. The ESF Second Position Paper on Public Procurement in Services, 25 November, 2002, www.esf.be.
22. Speech by John Prescott, 'The Partnership Approach: The UK Government Conference on Public-Private Partnerships', October, 2002, www.privatefinance-i.com.

Pensions of mass destruction

Richard Minns

Richard Minns argues that questions of welfare are inevitably overshadowed by questions of profit in private pension provision.

The title of this article is meant to signify that 'pensions' are not about abstract economic constructs concerned with ageing, demography, balance of public and private expenditure, savings ratios, dependency ratios. Instead pensions are the product of social economic and political forces. There is nothing 'objective' about pensions. They are a product of social conflict and concepts concerning the worth and income of different generations as determined by different social and economic interests. The implications of the issue present some important political and economic questions for us to consider. Here are some hypotheses:

♦ Privatisation of pensions is about the extension of certain financial interests concerning financial 'products' and stock markets. It is not about pensions or care and provision in old age (itself a problematic and political concept).
♦ Pensions, public and private, are a zero sum game. Privatisation is a *substitute* not a *complement* to public provision. There is no example anywhere in the world where both have increased together. Private provision is always at the expense of public provision.
♦ The implications of this are fundamental for the consideration of pensions 'reform'. Privatisation has enormous economic and structural consequences because it puts welfare issues under the responsibility of financial interests, for whom welfare is not a primary objective. Their objective is financial

product turnover, profit margins, and private financial expansion. Financial institutions are just that - financial institutions. They have diverse financial interests which have to support each other. It is impossible for a financial group to make a loss through the provision of 'welfare' if its logic for the group and its other activities is to make a profit from each and all of its operations. So the conundrum for the privatisation movement is how to make welfare profitable.

♦ Another 'zero-sum' issue can be seen in the observation that the structure and importance of financial systems in welfare provision goes hand-in-hand with the role of financial systems in the broader economy. It is difficult to find a stock-market dominated economy (i.e. high stock market total valuation as a percentage of national GDP) which coincides with a state dominated pension system (above average state or public pension expenditure as a percentage of GDP). Privatisation of pensions is about the nature of total economic structure, not about pensions.

♦ This entails the vital consideration of the broader financial implications of pensions privatisation. It is a matter of *who* controls the delivery, *how* they do this, and who gets most out of it - the deliverers or the supposed beneficiaries. If it is a question of welfare, it should be the latter. If it is not, it will be the former.

That this is an issue at whose heart lies the question of social and economic advantage between groups which have opposing interests could not be more clear. For example, what is the connection between the recent strikes and demonstrations over pension reform in France and Austria, and elsewhere, and - firstly - the enormous financial penalties on Wall Street investment banks such as Citigroup, Merrill Lynch and Goldman Sachs for manipulating investment research; secondly, the Enron scandal; thirdly, the failure of stakeholder pensions in the UK; and, finally, other financial scandals such as the reneging by Equitable Life and associated UK companies on their 'promises' to contributors and savers for future benefits?

The answer is that they are symptomatic of the simple financial interests behind the so-called provision of welfare - interests for which 'welfare' is actually secondary to corporate gain of one kind or another. For them it is another 'product' from which money is to be made. The end product is thus in total

Pensions of mass destruction

contradiction to the nature of the problem it aims to solve. The market is asked to resolve social problems caused by the self-same market.

The arguments for further reducing public provision of pensions, or for not relying on the state at all and instead extending private provision, are all - to a greater or lesser extent - based on a theory summarised by the World Bank in a seminal publication of 1994: *Averting the Old Age Crisis; Policies to Protect the Old AND Promote Growth*. Whatever the different national and local arguments for privatisation of pensions and the reduction of public provision, almost all the arguments can be traced back to the doomsday scenario depicted by this publication, of ageing populations, demographic timebombs, burdens of old people, crises of public expenditure, end of the welfare state as we have known it, and alleged crises in governments themselves

The World Bank argued, essentially, that cutting public expenditure and increasing private provision would lead to greater private savings, therefore greater private investment, therefore greater private production, greater GDP growth, and hence greater ability to pay for the increasing 'burden' of ageing societies. (It should, incidentally, be noted that many references to this publication have inadvertently omitted the emphasis on in its title on the word 'AND', which is the crucial connection in the Bank's theory of pensions and the economy.) Notwithstanding its wide citation and influence, however, no part of the Bank's theory has been proven. One revealing comment from a World Bank representative, analysing the results of the Bank's favourite exemplar of privatisation, namely Chile, concluded that:

> Closer inspection of the Chilean evidence indicates that the saving effect of the reform is not clear, and that the direct effect on private sector saving was perhaps negative. The strong rise in domestic saving was generated by strong public saving, more than balancing the direct fiscal costs of reform, and, perhaps, representing an inverse causality through which higher economic growth as a result of improved financial markets ... induced higher saving.[1]

Despite the lack of proof for the case, Holzmann argued that:

---

1. Robert Holzmann, *Pension Reform, Financial Market Development and Economic Growth*, IMF Working Paper WP/96/94, 1997, p214.

Nevertheless, for the emerging economies of Central and Eastern Europe, such a proof may not be necessary in order to follow a similar approach. What is important is that their financial markets are still underdeveloped, that pension funds may importantly accelerate their development if the required framework is established, and that developed financial markets can contribute to economic growth (p16).

Most of this of course involves mere supposition, as the qualifying vocabulary indicates.

Conversely, and based on fact rather than wishful thinking, the expansion of private financial markets also entails serious negative consequences. Consider the following. In 2003 eleven - mainly US - investment banks were fined a total of over $1.3 billion by the US SEC and other regulators, for manipulating research and information about corporate clients in order to retain lucrative banking business. Investment clients (pension funds and private clients) were duped into following investment advice based on questionable intelligence about investment ratings, and lost millions when the research turned out to be based on dubious data, without adequate foundation and supervision. Those fined included Citibank, Merrill Lynch, Credit Suisse-First Boston, and Goldman Sachs - who also, between them, manage billions of pension fund money.

Four of those fined were in the top ten of UK pension managers, and were fined $470 million between them. These four (Merrill Lynch, Union Bank of Switzerland, Goldman Sachs and Deutsche Bank) manage nearly £100 billion of pension fund money in the UK, and no less than one and a quarter trillion (thousand billion) of funds worldwide. They are among the largest one hundred companies in the world as measured by market capitalisation. Two are also the subject of a private lawsuit for their activities in allegedly supporting the apartheid regime in South Africa. (And the others involved in the lawsuit include Barclays, the largest pension fund manager in the UK and number 73 of the largest companies in the world, Citigroup, the sixth largest company in the world, Credit Suisse First Boston (number 143), and JPMorgan (number 54) (all also fined by the US Securities and Exchange Commission for the manipulation of investment research for fund clients)).

The sole point here is to indicate that in any discussion of private responsibility for pensions provision, there are likely to be other beneficiary and social issues which some may want to be taken into account. The targets, or memoranda and articles of association, of the private companies that offer pensions do not, as a matter of course, include the provision of social welfare. My argument is solely concerned with looking at the power of different social and economic interests in the determination and implementation of pensions provision, and the various implications of this for beneficiaries and non-beneficiaries.

Another problem that can arise from corporate pension provision was seen in the placing by Enron of millions of dollars of employees' future pension provision into the company's own shares, which then became worthless through its failed financial engineering.

Next, financial advisers and managers in the UK find stakeholder pensions difficult because, at a controlled fee of 1 per cent, they cannot make enough of a margin out of the business to make it worthwhile. So, in order to get the turnover to make the margin worthwhile, they have gone up-market to higher income groups, rather than targeting the lower income groups who were the whole purpose of the project.

What's more, the UK has a current surplus of over £17 billion in its social insurance fund (as of 2002), the main purpose of which is to pay state pensions, which have declined in value by over 30% in twenty years. Meanwhile the public subsidy to private pension providers in tax relief is between £13 and 20 billion per year - and their managed funds have increased by over 1000% in the same period. Campbell concludes that the UK state pension is not more expensive than private provision.[2] The £30 billion annual cost of the state pension is the gross outgoing from the national insurance fund; this is not a cost to the exchequer, since all of it is met by the fund from its own income sources. She also points out that the state pension, through the surplus in the national insurance fund, arguably makes a net contribution to the British government's exchequer account.

A further scandal in the UK has been the widespread mis-selling of private pensions, which cost the government £15 billion in promotion, tax concessions and rebates, and led to over half a million people losing benefits of one kind or

---

2. Mary Campbell, 'Redressing the Balance', *The Political Quarterly*, Vol. 69, No 1, January-March 1998

another. Then there was the failure of major insurance companies such as Equitable Life to deliver on their promises to endowment holders and pension savers, when they unilaterally changed the rules of policy entitlement.

And now we have seen the announcement by BT and Royal Mail pension funds (together the largest pension fund in the UK) that they have a 'black hole' of over £10 billion, because of the fall in stock markets. This occurred in the context of the decline of total UK private funds (of over £600 billion) by £100 billion from their previous year, for the same reason. In other words, there is no abstract economics about pensions. It is about who controls what, what they then invest in, and who pays when they fail for pensioners and beneficiaries.

Any research - in Europe, Latin America, Eastern Europe, North America and elsewhere - needs to consider the role of financial markets, the implications for financial and industrial organisation, and the overall concepts of welfare and pensions.

The essential point is that arguments about savings and investment will not produce a formula for greater economic growth and the ability to pay for pensions, as many would like. The problem is that the privatisation of pensions leads us into monetary growth (and decline), not real growth. When stock markets decline, or savings decline in value, or pensions decline in value - all the same thing - despite public subsidy, the object of the privatisation is seriously undermined.

But this is the hypothesis: financial institutions have as their objective not the delivery of welfare but the production of sufficient margin to make the delivery of welfare as a product sufficiently attractive to sell. The concept of 'margin' is crucial, and defines the private assessment of welfare. The 'welfare state' thus becomes the 'margin state'.

So why 'pensions of mass destruction'? The reason is this. The liabilities of present state-dominated regimes in many countries are not the reason for the current debate. And while the search for the elusive proof of the threat of state-run systems continues, the question of private financial economic interests and their side-effects is ignored, and the problems they cause are treated as temporary aberrations. Yet the issues involved are fundamental in terms of economic and social forces. These are the forces which should be the subject of academic analysis, not the arguments for pension 'reform' per se. This is a political and economic issue about social and economic forces, and who really benefits. There is nothing abstract and neutral about pensions, and nothing abstract and neutral about financial markets.

This article is based on a paper presented to the Conference on 'Privatisation of Public Pension Systems - Forces, Experience, Prospects', Vienna 19-21 June 2003, organised by EpoC (Improvement of Economic Policy Coordination for Full Employment and Social Cohesion in Europe).

Social democracy in Britain and Europe

Interview with Renzio Imbeni

Renzo Imbeni is a Vice-President of the European Parliament and an MEP for the Democratici di Sinistra (DS, Left Democrats), the largest successor party to the Italian Communist Party. The DS is also the largest party in the Ulivo ('Olive Tree') centre-left coalition and was in government between 1996-2001, when comparisons were made with New Labour's modernisation agenda. The main achievement of this government, led initially by Romano Prodi, was the creation of favourable conditions for entry into the Euro. Since its heavy defeat in 2001, when the Berlusconi government was elected, a major discussion has opened in the DS over its future political strategy, one that has been influenced by interventions from the film director Nanni Moretti and the rise of Sergio Cofferati, the former leader of the CGIL, Italy's biggest trade union

federation. Subsequently the Italian left has undergone something of a revival, following massive demonstrations against the suspension of article 18 of the Italian constitution (thereby making it easier for employers to dismiss workers), the rapid rise of 'No (now 'New') Global' and the social forum movement, and opposition to the Iraq war. Recent election results have also shown strong gains for the centre-left. Imbeni is also a member of the Bureau of the Socialist Group in the European Parliament and a former Mayor of Bologna (1983-1993). Here he is interviewed by Geoff Andrews.

What is your view on the current post-Iraq global political situation?

It is not an easy situation. The United Nations is now weaker than before. The relationship between Europe and the US is also in a bad way. I think the relationship between the two biggest democracies in the world will be of crucial importance for the future. The responsibility for this negative situation lies with the strategy of the Bush administration. I refer to the document of 17.9.2002 signed by President Bush. This was a completely new and different strategy, not only from that of President Clinton, but also from all US presidents since 1945. The strategy of a pre-emptive war and unilateral war is so clear in the document. The document states that the US can declare war alone, without any need of alliances and before the enemy can attack.

I think there are two points to this strategy that we, as Europeans, need to reflect upon. The first is that the situation is very different from the Cold War, where you had countries with nuclear weapons such as the Soviet Union. Now the threat is terrorism. We have to understand this better. There was a very big difference in the reaction to 9/11. Everybody was shocked. But our shock in Europe was not comparable to that of the US. It is a mistake to underestimate this. I always use the example of my city Bologna after the terrorist bomb at the station in August 1980 when 85 people were killed. Two months later, the extreme right-wing party decided to ask for the re-introduction of the death penalty and many democrats on the left agreed because of the shock of the bombing.

The second point is that there are many countries that have no democracy and many dictatorships continue. We cannot believe this situation will last forever. On this point, in the Bush document, one of the key words is the need for 'action'. The need to take action against dictatorship and for democracy is stressed. However, the conclusions of Bush are completely unacceptable for us. As Europeans, in the European Union, there is now the need for an alternative strategy on global security, not in competition with the US, but a different strategy. There may be similarities in some of the analysis, but not in the conclusions. Not unilateralism, but multilateralism; not war but peace.

There are also big differences in our histories which it is important to recognise in the different positions taken on the Gulf War. For Europeans, in particular for continental Europeans, peace is a value. It is not just an objective. For the US, and also to a large degree, the UK, peace is one of two options. For countries such as Italy, France and Germany, war was a reality in order to overcome fascism and Nazism. For us war was a consequence of fascism. For Germany it was the consequence of Nazism. In Europe, war was the decision of the dictator. At the end of the second world war we said 'never again'. Also the participation of the partisans and the resistance in the war in parts of Italy and France was a necessity, not a choice. For us it is impossible to imagine that you can export democracy through war.

How concerned are you about the current relationship between the UK and the US?

I think the UK, as a member of the European Union but also with a 'special relationship' to the US, has found itself in the middle of the river. For many of us, the UK's position on the war was a deception. It is true that in the treaty of the European Union there are no juridical obligations, but there are some articles in the existing treaty where it is stated that before we take our decision as an international body to go to war, it is better to have a co-ordinated foreign policy. We know that Tony Blair decided on his position without the use of these articles.

Were you surprised by Blair's position?

No, I was not surprised because of the different history of the UK. I was surprised by the manner that he adopted, rather than the content, because we had the impression that he was, if I can say it, the 'master' of Bush.

How damaging do you think the differences over the Iraq war will be for the future of the European Left? There are also differences, for example, between the UK and other countries over the inclusion of social rights in the new European constitution. In addition

Blair has increasingly allied himself with Berlusconi and Aznar on flexible labour markets and other social policy areas.

I don't know if the divisions over the war will be more significant for the future of the European Left than the divisions over social policy. We were surprised by the agreements between Blair and Berlusconi over flexible labour markets. We need to reflect on the new global strategy, and also the common social policy. The key point in analysing the British situation is that Blair became the Prime Minister after the Thatcher Governments, and Thatcher completely changed the social infrastructure of the UK.

Some of my colleagues in the European Socialist Group are now arguing that there are different values between Europe and the US. I don't agree. They talk about Kyoto and Guantanamo Bay. In these cases you can say 'you are violating your constitution'. The restrictions on the freedom of the press during the war were unbelievable. My daughter lives in San Francisco. She told me that it is impossible to find a different viewpoint on the TV or in the newspapers. There is no real debate. But this is so strange in the history of the United States, with its constitution. It is not enough to conclude that the US has different values.

The role of the European Union in my view is to make policies to change, if it is possible, the strategy of the US administration. Of course the decision is in the hands of European voters next year, but we also need to think of the other side of the Atlantic.

What about the strategy of the socialist group in the European Parliament?

All the positions we took in the socialist group about the war, before the beginning of the war, were unanimous. The Labour MEPs agreed with our position, which was that we needed the decision of the United Nations. The socialist group agreed unanimously on this point.

On 21 January we also voted on a resolution in the Plenary of the European Parliament which stated that there were no reasons at that moment to attack Iraq. This was also the position of the socialist group. After the beginning of the war, the majority (not all) of the Labour MEPs in our group changed their position. They also tried to convince us that there was a legal basis for war.

And were you convinced?

Not at all.

When Tony Blair arrived in Italy to seek the support of the Italian government for the war, [Francesco] Rutelli [leader of the Centre-left Ulivo coalition] and [Massimo] D'Alema [former DS Prime Minister] tried to dissuade him. They told him the war was a mistake. Many, including *La Repubblica* [Italian centre-left daily], saw this meeting as the end of the 'third way' – if you like, the British model for the European left.

I don't really know what the 'third way' is. If you say that we need a left that is more in favour of opportunities for young people, for guarantees for universal services for school, health and other public services, such as gas and electricity, then the key thing is that everybody has to be in a condition to use public services. I don't know if the third way will guarantee rights to health, social protection and access to schools. These are fundamental rights in the history of social democracy and therefore crucial to the Charter in the second part of the new European Constitution.

In Europe the left is in a difficult situation. When the participation of the people in public life is decreasing, it is a very negative situation for the left, a problem that is more important for the left than for the right. In Europe and Italy, in local, national and European elections, we see a decreasing participation. After Seattle, with the movements against one kind of globalisation and, in the last three months the opposition to the war in Italy and other countries, this was a positive demonstration for me. One part of our young people is getting involved in public life. In the beginning it was not clear in the Italian movement what would be the attitude towards violence. But in Genoa, after Carlo Giuliani was killed, a clear position was developed in the movement against violence. Now the movement is big. I think the roots of the new politics of the left are here, in these movements for a new kind of globalisation and against war.

No Global was the beginning of the movement, and while I understand the need in the early part of a movement to state a clear position, to be 'anti-global' is not possible, as 'global' is a reality. Now the movement has matured and it describes itself as '*New Global*'.

This is a very different view from New Labour, which has consistently opposed the politics of the new movements.

In the last (local, Scottish and Welsh) elections in the UK friends told me that the Labour Party lost seats to the Scottish Socialist Party, Liberal Democrats and Greens. We have to ask why? Because of the foreign policy on fish? The new regional policies? No. The problem was the war and the attitude of the Labour Government towards the movements against the war and this kind of globalisation.

How would you assess the current state of the Italian Left?

In Italy the left is stronger than two years ago. After the election in 2001, it was in a very dangerous situation. We have to find an equilibrium between the ideas of the new movements - our members are an important part of the new movements - and the ability to provide a credible alternative to the Berlusconi government.

What effect have the interventions of Sergio Cofferati and Nanni Moretti had on the Italian left?

It was a provocative moment when Moretti told the leaders of the Italian centre-left (in 2002) that 'we will never win with you'. After he said this, there were two possible responses. One was to say that he was not a politician and that he should go back to the cinema, and one of the Ulivo leaders said this. In my view this was not an intelligent answer. The answer of Fassino [leader of the DS] was: 'we have to talk'. I think this was an intelligent response, because at this moment we needed to re-engage with civil society, in a Gramscian way.

Cofferati has emerged over the last two years as a leader in the fight against the Berlusconi government to keep article 18 [the statute of the constitution which safeguards jobs]. He decided in that first moment to be strong and hard in the fight against Berlusconi. This also allowed him as a leader to make a positive link with the anti-war movements and the political parties. He has been moved by events. As a leader you cannot always take the direction you originally intend, but need to respond to the people's views. I think this is why he went with the position on the war of 'senza se, senza ma' ('without ifs, without buts'), whereas in reality, for me and probably for Cofferati, there always many ifs and many buts. We have to remember the movement against the war was very diverse.

We have to explain that we cannot accept only one kind of globalisation and we cannot accept war. We need less exclusion and more inclusion in the social spheres and more investment in human capital. We also have to demonstrate to everyone that we are a responsible left. We must convince the Italian people that they can have confidence in us.

Snatching defeat from the jaws of victory

Britain and the euro

George Irvin

George Irvin analyses the government's failure of nerve on the euro.

On 9 June 2003, the Chancellor announced that Britain had once again failed four of the five 'economic tests' for euro-entry. While New Labour scrambles frantically to paper over the cracks, the euro debate has become emblematic of Britain's increasingly uneasy relationship with the EU, a relationship strained by years of indecision about economic and political integration, damaged by Britain's alliance with the US during the Iraq war and, most recently, poisoned by the tabloid press campaign against the draft Constitution. In 1997, the newly elected Labour government appeared to be the very antithesis of the Euro-phobic wing of the Tory Party. But, while remaining rhetorically pro-European, Labour has shifted steadily rightward; today, its European pronouncements recall the flag-waving chauvinism of the Thatcher-Major years. Indeed, a significant segment of the British left is euro-sceptic. The spectrum includes unreconstructed Bennites, a new generation of militant trade unionists, and disillusioned Blairites whose allegiance is now shifting to Gordon Brown. The implications of remaining semi-detached from Europe are worrying. While the current article is about the economics of euro-membership, the underlying question remains one about the geo-politics of the EU. Britain cannot stand still; it must either move forward within Europe or drift further into the mid-Atlantic, ultimately into the neo-liberal grasp of the Unites States. Starkly put, the choice for Britain is between European social democracy and US-style neo-liberal capitalism.

Below, I try to put the economic debate over the euro in a manner accessible to the non-specialist. I first consider Gordon Brown's 'five tests', to which the verdict on 9 June was 'no, not yet ... though perhaps in the not too distant future'. In the following section, I counter some of the arguments against joining, and put what I consider to be the main arguments in favour, as well as what the UK can do once 'in' to help reform eurozone economic policy. In the third section I review what has rightly been described as the 'sixth test', notably, the opportunity cost of not joining the Euro at the earliest opportunity.

The 'five tests'

As everyone knows by now, the 'five tests' were hastily concocted by Gordon Brown at the Treasury in October 1997 shortly after Labour came to power, and which EMU (Economic and Monetary Union) at that time was deemed to fail. Few non-specialists, though, are clear what the tests were and are, even after the verdict on 9 June. Briefly resumed, they are as follows.

- *Convergence*: it must be shown that Britain's interest rates are sufficiently close to those of the eurozone, and its exchange rate sufficiently competitive such that entry will not harm the UK economy. More generally, Britain's business cycle cannot be too far out of line with that of the main eurozone countries if eurozone interest and exchange rates are to remain appropriate.
- *Flexibility*: this means 'labour market flexibility'. Joining the euro means that Britain can no longer devalue and that the weight of adjusting to any loss of competitiveness vis-à-vis the eurozone would fall exclusively on wages. Unless productivity rises, UK wages must be flexible enough to bear the burden.
- *Investment*: will Britain's membership of the euro help or hinder investment, in particular so-called 'inward investment', i.e. the flow of DFI (direct foreign investment) into the UK from the rest of the world?
- *Financial services*: will joining the euro help or hinder the growth of the financial services sector (i.e. the City)?

♦ *Growth and jobs*: it must be shown that joining the euro would enhance - or at least not stifle - economic growth and job creation. Given the current stagnation of the main eurozone economies, this test seen by some as the most contentious. Their argument is that a one-size fits-all interest rate and the SGP (Stability and Growth Pact) would harm Britain.

Today, as in 1997, the Treasury's view is that euro-entry passes one test clearly, that of helping the financial services sector to grow. On all other tests, the verdict is either negative or wary. Broadly speaking, on *convergence*, the conventional argument is that the UK business cycle continues to be more closely aligned with that of the US than Germany and France. In 1997 the pound was too high relative to the (then) DM - indeed it had appreciated after 1992 - and Britain's interest rate was still several percentage points higher than that of its continental counterparts. The current Treasury view is that there is closer symmetry of the UK and eurozone economies today, that the pound is very nearly competitively aligned with the euro and that interest rates are converging. Nevertheless, the Chancellor remains unwilling to say that the degree of convergence is sufficient. Indeed he has introduced a new argument: because UK mortgages are variable and linked to short-term interest rates, house price swings are greater in the UK than in other EU countries. He therefore proposes to move to the system of fixed rate mortgages based on long-term interest rates. Long rates in Britain and the eurozone are broadly in line, but this changeover will take time, we are told.

The *flexibility* test is a curious one. If the euro is adopted, a fixed exchange rate (within the eurozone) will prevail leaving adjustment to any external shock - what economists call an 'exogenous shock' - dependent on flexible wage rates and growing productivity. While Britain claims to have Europe's most flexible labour markets, low productivity growth and the overvaluation of the pound since the late 1990s until quite recently has been such that UK manufacturing has declined more sharply during this period than at any time since the Thatcher years.[1] Since the pound has recently fallen and

---

1. In May 2000, the GBP peaked at DEM 3.46, nearly 20 per cent above the value at which it was forced to leave the ERM in1992. Huhne estimates that between 1998 and 2000 when the pound peaked, British manufacturing lost 350,000 jobs. See J. Forder, and C. Huhne, *Both Sides of the Coin*, Profile Books, London 2001, p14.

labour productivity has improved slightly, the current Treasury argument has changed. Instead of asking whether Britain is flexible enough, the Treasury seems to be asking whether the rest of Europe - notably Germany - is flexible enough? Clearly Gordon Brown and his experts think not, and much is now made of the need for the EU to reform its labour market along UK lines; i.e. employers' indirect labour costs should be lower, they should be able to shed labour more easily and the jobless should be encouraged, in Norman Tebbitt's infamous phrase, to 'get on their bikes and find work'. The implicit assumption is that, were Britain to join, it might catch the German disease, either because of increased trade union power or of the 'deflationary' bias of EU spending caps (see below).

On the *investment* question, Treasury reactions are mixed. On the one hand, it is accepted that long-term inward investment will suffer if Britain remains out of the euro permanently. On the other, while most analysts concede that inward investment has fallen somewhat in the recent past, some euro-sceptics argue that it is still to early to tell whether Britain is losing strategically important investment; equally, these same people argue that the UK should look for strategic partnerships elsewhere; eg, in the US or in the high-growth Asian economies. Gordon Brown apparently accepts that it is still too early to tell.

As to the *financial sector* test, this was passed in 1997 and again in 2003. What has changed, though, is that the City has continued to prosper despite Britain's retention of the pound. Economists are divided between those who think the euro is now largely irrelevant to Britain's financial sector, and those who argue that just as New York could not act as America's financial centre were it not part of the dollar-zone, so London cannot be Europe's financial centre wile remaining outside the eurozone.

The final 'test' is about *growth and jobs*. As in the case of the labour market flexibility test, since 1997 this test has been reversed. While Brown has conceded that joining the euro will bring Britain more trade, the Treasury's conventional view is that since Britain does better than the eurozone on growth and jobs, to join the euro might put Britain's performance at risk - at least until such time as the eurozone undertakes the necessary reforms. A minority argues that although Britain has in recent years outperformed the eurozone on average, the smaller eurozone countries currently outperform Britain on growth (Eire, Greece), as do several on job creation. In particular, critics of the Treasury view point out that UK growth has been led by high levels of consumer spending associated with the house-price boom, that the UK trade deficit has worsened, and that UK industrial growth is negative and close to bottom of the EU-15 league table.[2]

Some pro-euro economists argue that Britain has, on recently published Treasury evidence, passed the five tests - the problem is rather that New Labour lacks the courage of its convictions.[3] Most economists - including many Euro-sceptics - would agree that the 'five tests' are arbitrary and incomplete; this is one reason why the tests were supplemented and 1738 pages of documents were distributed to Cabinet Ministers. Equally, there has been much debate about what constitutes 'sufficient' evidence for a test to be passed or failed.

Looking at the wider debate, there are at least two main questions which, strictly speaking, are either not addressed or addressed only indirectly by the June assessment. First, the related questions of whether abandoning the pound matters and - most importantly - whether the Maastricht Treaty of 1992 imparts a deflationary bias to the eurozone economy. Second, what are the benefits foregone of staying out; i.e. does remaining in mid-Atlantic carry a significant opportunity cost?

Arguments about joining
Does abandoning the pound matter?
To readers of the *Sun* or the *Daily Mail*, having the sovereign's head on our banknotes clearly does matter; indeed, for some diehard euro-sceptics, no possible evidence can be adduced which would tilt the balance in favour of the euro. Debate at this level is clearly pointless. The concerned but undecided reader will presumably want to consider a less symbolic balancing of costs and benefits; for example to consider whether the loss of control over our exchange and interest rates in favour of 'one size fits all' is not a genuine cost; or whether the costs of conversion to the euro will be outweighed by transaction costs saved; whether the economy will be less prone to exchange-rate shocks, and so on.

---

2. For the 2002 figures by quarter from Eurostat , see www.ibeurope.com/Database/5800/5960.htm; see also Ray Barrell and Martin Weale, 'Designing and Choosing Macroeconomic Frameworks: The Position of the UK after 4 years of the Euro', NIESR Discussion Paper No.212, 19 April 2003.
3. See Will Hutton's excellent piece 'I've been betrayed on the euro', *Observer*, 8.6.03.

Soundings

If Britain abandons the pound, it loses control over its exchange rate and, by logical extension, over its interest rate.[4] Much has been made of this point by the anti-euro camp; by contrast, many pro-euro economists argue that interest rate and exchange rate autonomy in the UK has, over the long term, been a bad thing. Looking at the 30-year period 1966-96, the pound fell from DEM 11 to DEM 2.3 - a relative fall of 5 per cent per annum - while in terms of labour productivity and GDP growth, Britain remained well behind Germany.[5] To appreciate this argument one must look at Britain's vulnerability to exchange rate movements and the relative weakness of interest-rate policy.

Until the price of gold was freed in 1971 and fixed exchanged rates collapsed in 1973, exchange rates were not set by the market and nor was monetary policy the main instrument of macroeconomic policy. The Thatcher-Reagan years - combined with the internationalisation of capital markets - changed all that. Today's conventional wisdom says that the exchange rate is set by the international market and government uses the interest rate to steer the economy through the business cycle and offset the effect of unanticipated external shocks (e.g. a sudden rise in oil prices).[6]

The problem with this sort of textbook economics is that in a world of speculative capital flows, exchange rates are unstable and tend to over- or undershoot their equilibrium level.[7] Nor can Central Banks always intervene successfully to keep the exchange rate at the desired level, as 16 September 1992 ('Black Wednesday') showed, when an overvalued pound was forced out of the ERM (Exchange Rate Mechanism). In the intervening years, massive capital flows have produced further financial crises in Latin America and Southeast Asia.[8] Most recently, after years of defying gravity, the

---

4. Note that Britain does not lose full control since, as a major EU economy, Britain's economic performance influences that of the eurozone and Britain gains a voice
5. See Currie, quoted in *Both Sides of the Coin*, p71.
6. By 'interest rate' is meant the short-term interest rate on monetary instruments, itself closely aligned with the rate at which the Central Bank will lend to the commercial banking sector.
7. The 'equilibrium level' is best thought of as that exchange rate at which domestic prices would be closely aligned with world prices such that purchasing power parity (PPP) would be achieved; i.e. a hamburger would cost the same in New York, London and Buenos Aires. For the pound the 'equilibrium' is thought to be in the region of 1.37 euros.

overvalued dollar has fallen 25 per cent against the euro in 18 months and threatens to go dangerously lower.[9] Because over 50 per cent of Britain's visible trade is with the EU (versus 17 per cent with the USA), large exchange rate fluctuations between sterling and the euro are undesirable. As long as the UK holds on to sterling, UK investment in the eurozone will carry exchange rate risk and a higher rate of return on such investment will be sought. Since sterling's value has fallen relative to the euro (GBP 1 = EUR 1.40 at the time of writing), the objection that Britain might join the euro at 'an uncompetitive exchange rate' is no longer sustainable. But no one can be certain what sterling's rate will be in five year's time. Exchange rate fluctuations against the currency of our major trading partners carry a real cost in terms of risk. If sterling's value is left to the mercy of an increasingly volatile capital market, the magnitude of exchange rate fluctuations will almost certainly rise in future.

The 'one-size-fits-all' objection to adhering to a eurozone interest rate is equally problematic. Opponents of the euro often conflate two arguments. The first concerns how far the interest rate matters. First-year economics students learn about what Keynes called the 'liquidity trap'; namely, the fact that when an economy is in recession, lowering the interest rate to near zero does not help much. The example of Japan, which has experienced nearly a decade of zero growth despite having the lowest interest rate of the industrialised countries, is instructive. The same misleading belief in the power of interest rates informs the argument of those who proclaim that Germany's poor performance is due entirely to the excessively monetary stringency of the Bundesbank after reunification in 1990 and, more recently, the 'conservative' monetary stance of

---

8. After Norman Lamont began shadowing the DEM in 1987, the new Chancellor, John Major, took the pound into the ERM in 1990 at DEM 2.95, a rate which most analysts considered too high. The 1991 recession convinced international markets that the rate was unsustainable and by late 1992 the position became untenable. Like Britain, Italy was forced to leave the ERM in 1992, but renegotiated its exchange rate and rejoined. The Bundesbank had suggested Britain might renegotiate before 'Black Wednesday', but this warning went unheeded by the Treasury; after the event, such was the embarrassment that the Treasury remained firmly opposed to the ERM and its successor, the single currency.
9. Interestingly, the Fed has shown no signs of wanting to halt dollar depreciation, leading a number of countries to conclude that the US is 'exporting' its unsustainable external account deficit, which could otherwise only be cut by reducing US domestic demand (absorption).

Soundings

the ECB (European Central Bank) and its lack of transparency. While Germany has a supply side problem of a high reservation wage and an over-regulated service sector, Germany's main problem is too low a level of aggregate demand.[10] (The question of the ECB's monetary stringency is dealt with below.) Growth depends essentially on rising productivity, and productivity cannot rise while growth prospects look bleak and investment remains stagnant.

On a minor note, the Treasury now argues that by entering the euro and adopting lower short-term interest rates, the house-price boom would get out of control. This is because, unlike the rest of the EU, in Britain mortgage rates are tied to short-term rates, which fluctuate far more than long-rates; this is sometimes called the 'variable rate mortgage' problem. This argument ignores several crucial facts. First, the house price boom has already peaked in most parts of Britain. Second, the difference in short-term rates between the UK and the eurozone is only 175 basis points, while the difference in long-term rates is negligible; even were Britain to enter the euro tomorrow, it is unlikely that building societies would lower their mortgage rates by more than 1 per cent. Thirdly, the house price boom and consumer credit can be reined in by other means; a temporary increase in duties on conveyancing would be one such measure. Most important, moving to a continental-style or *Pfandbrief* system would be a good thing since current UK mortgage finance forces households to accept large risks: when short-term interest rates to squeeze an inflationary boom, households face higher debt at precisely the time house prices are falling. This in turn makes Government reluctant to tighten monetary policy, weakening the usefulness of monetary policy. Thus, while accepting that lower ECB short-term interest rates would ease the burden of risk on house-owners and reduce the volatility of the house price market, it is nonsense to suggest that entering the euro would lead to a house-price led inflationary boom. The minor fixes required to contain the 'house-price boom' can easily be accomplished before entry, while the full shift to fixed-rate mortgages can be accomplished after entry. Besides, even assuming (quite unrealistically) that a referendum was held in 2004, it would take three

---

10. See James Forder in *Both Sides of the Coin*. Forder overlooks the fact that since unification it is estimated that Germany has spent 4-5 per cent of its annual GDP in maintaining East German living standards.

years of preparation after a 'yes' vote to adopt the new currency. Britain would join in 2007 at the earliest!

Is the euro deflationary?

The most serious argument is that the eurozone suffers from an in-built 'deflationary bias'. This is because the ECB's brief set out in the Maastricht Treaty is to keep inflation in the range 0-2 per cent. In this it differs both from the US Federal Reserve - which is charged with finding a trade-off between the goals of combating inflation and maintaining employment - and from the BoE (Bank of England). The latter, although unconstrained by any full-employment goal, has a so-called 'symmetrical' target of 2.5 per cent inflation; i.e. should inflation falls below 2 ½ per cent, the BoE must loosen monetary policy. Furthermore, the UK can at present use more active fiscal policy to offset any weakness on the monetary side, whereas the SGP (Stability and Growth Pact) signed in 1997 imposes fines on those countries running a fiscal deficit grater than 3 per cent of cyclically-adjusted GDP.

I accept the 'deflationary bias' argument, as indeed do many supporters of the euro - most notably the current President of the Commission, Romano Prodi and his Trade Commissioner, Pascal Lamy. The 2 per cent inflation limit, the 3 per cent budget-deficit cap and the fiscal borrowing constraint (debt cannot exceed 60 per cent of GDP) were dreamt up in the late 1980s when the Community was still struggling with an inflationary legacy. The danger today, however, is not inflation but rather its opposite, deflation. The Council of Ministers has, in effect, ignored attempts by the Commission to impose SGP rules on Germany and France. Even the ex-President of the *Bundesbank*, Karl-Otto Pohl said at a conference in late 2002 that in the EU 'the main problems are stagnation or even a recession' (*Observer*, 24.11.02). As German growth turns negative, US interest rates fall to Japanese levels and the Bush 'stimulus package' attempts to redistribute income in the wrong direction, a veritable chorus of academic and business economists are urging both the US and the EU to abandon pre-Keynesian orthodoxy and adopt actively expansionary monetary *and* fiscal policy.

Because of the manner in which Britain calculates inflation, the 2½ per cent inflation target used by the BoE is tighter than the 2 per cent used by the ECB. This is not to deny that the ECB needs to loosen the rules: symmetrical inflation targeting would be useful, but there is nothing sacrosanct about 2 per cent. Doubling the ECB inflation target would not lead to hyperinflation in the current world deflationary climate. It would allow the ECB to lower interest rates and well as to act more pro-actively. Neither the Maastricht budget deficit cap of 3 per cent nor the 60 per cent borrowing rule need be carved in stone. The '3/60 rule' was devised in the run up to EMU before 1999, when separate EU currencies were still vulnerable to speculation. Financial markets needed to believe the euro would work. A relatively conservative reform would be to make the 3 per cent GDP cap refer to the core, not the headline budget; i.e. to the budget deficit stripped of its cyclical component. And as in the UK, the deficit should exclude capital spending.[11] There is no reason why a higher deficit cap should not be allowed as long as inflation does not rise unduly. The US total budget deficit is currently forecast to be 4 per cent in 2003 and rising (3 per cent if only the federal deficit is counted). Moreover, in contrast to the EU, where domestic private saving is high, the US internal deficit is mirrored by a growing external trade deficit.

Gordon Brown's mounting of the moral pulpit, to extol the virtues of Anglo-Saxon pragmatism in creating jobs and overcoming the 'structural rigidities' which plague our EU neighbours, while continuing to veto British euro-entry, is, from the point of view of those within the eurozone who hope to change the rules, counterproductive. It is likely that the debate over the SGP and ECB rules will be settled before the complement of 10 new members is fully achieved. Britain has a short window of opportunity in which to put its position. By staying out, Britain cannot hope to influence that debate, just as happened with the Common Agricultural Policy in the 1960s.

Equally important is the issue of fiscal reform. Consider both EU level and national level. At EU level, although the 'federal' budget is a tiny 1.1 per cent of combined EU GDP, nearly half is spent on the CAP (Common Agricultural Policy).[12] With enlargement imminent, though, CAP spending will slowly fall in real terms after 2006, thus freeing EU 'federal' funds for other uses. The most pressing need of the EU is for greater regional equity; and though such equity

---

11. The UK Treasury's 'golden rule' is more conservative: it says that over the cycle current revenue should cover current expenditure, so restricting long-term public borrowing exclusively for capital expenditure.
12. This figure is capped by the Maastricht Treaty at 1.27 per cent.

can be achieved in part through the regional policies of member states, ultimately much will depend upon enlarging the Structural Fund and putting money into improved EU-wide economic and social infrastructure.[13] Some years ago, the MacDougall Committee reported to the Commission that if there were to be ongoing redistribution from rich to poor regions - rather than merely in compensation for shocks - the EU budget would need to rise to somewhere between 2-7 per cent of EU GDP. As European anti-federalists have gained the upper hand in recent years, this proposal has been consigned to oblivion. Fiscally induced reflation must thus rely on the relatively weak mechanism of inter-Government fiscal co-ordination.

At national level, fiscal reform is required if the 'social market economy' is to have any meaning. While much current discussion is devoted to cutting 'unaffordable' expenditure on pensions, unemployment benefit, medical services and so on, few political parties (even on the left) have called for the higher tax levels required to finance an 'affordable' level of public spending compatible with maintaining a social market economy under conditions of increasing demographic strain. The tax burden differs greatly between the different member states: from about 50 per cent in France to 33 per cent in Eire (slightly lower than the UK), and this is precisely what lies at the heart of the 'tax harmonisation' debate. If the inclusive nature of social benefits is not to be eroded, 'tax competition' must be minimised and the tax-burden question must be debated as an EU-wide issue, and not merely one of national competence.

The opportunity costs of not joining

Although the UK has not joined the euro, at present it is considered a 'pre-in' country to use the jargon. As Begg *et al* point out, saying 'no' to entry can mean two things.[14] Either it means 'not yet but the tests will be re-examined soon', in which case Britain's 'pre-in' status may be retained for a time; or it means 'no and probably not any time soon', in which case the UK would become a 'probable

---

13. Thus Jacques Delors, when European Commissioner in the early 1990s, proposed a trans-European transport plan emphasising a network of high-speed rail links to take the strain off air and road traffic; the plan was rejected for reasons of budgetary orthodoxy.
14. David Begg, Olivier Blanchard *et al*, 'The Consequences of saying no', Britain in Europe, London May 2003.

out'. Although the 9 June announcement was interpreted as 'not yet' rather than 'never', the number of tests deemed 'passed' was one of five - no better than in 1997. What is certain is that the longer Britain waits to hold a referendum, the less likely are other trading partners to believe Britain will join. How is this likely to effect British trade with Europe, its share of inward investment and, ultimately, its growth?

One of the oldest pro-euro points is that by joining, Britain avoids the costs of exchange rate conversion. As the story goes, back in the 1990s, if one started out from London with £100 and changed the entire amount into local currency each time one crossed the border into another EU country, one would return to London with only £50. The transactions cost argument is correct, but of course relatively trivial. Far more important is that membership of a large single currency area like the eurozone gives companies the chance to trade in a single market and enjoy the scale and technological economies so long available to industry in the USA. Moreover, there is quite compelling evidence that given the option of trading within the currency area (intra-trade) and outside it, intra-trade will generally win. Several studies have examined the case of Canadian provinces trading with each other compared to trading with US states across the border; the results suggest that a Canadian province is twenty times more likely to do business with another province than with an equidistant US state.[15] Begg et al conclude that 'there is now robust evidence that monetary unions do foster trade between their member states' (p10), and that the principal cost for Britain of staying out would be its failure to share in the growth of intra-trade together with its failure to benefit from rising competitiveness.

The evidence on intra-EU trade is that Britain has already lost out. If one considers British, German and French trade with other EU countries in 1998 and 2001 (i.e. before and after the launch of the euro), Germany and France both raised their share of trade in GDP - from 27 to 32 per cent and 28 to 32 per cent respectively - while Britain's trade share fell from 23 to 22 per cent. Britain's share of FDI (foreign direct investment) into the EU also fell: from an average of 39 per cent over the period 1990-98 to 24 per cent for 1999-2001. If

---

15. See, for example, J. McCallum, 'National borders matter: Canada-US regional trade patterns', *American Economic Review* 1995.

one considers labour productivity - output per hour worked - Britain has lost out even more sharply; its productivity level in 2002 was 15 per cent lower than the average of Germany and France.[16]

A further benefit of EMU is that it creates greater market integration within member states. The argument in Britain about *convergence* has tended to ask: is Britain's economy sufficiently like the rest of the EU to make entry advisable? Here, the empirical evidence has been mixed: Britain's cycle has not fully converged with the core countries, but it is certainly more similar to the EU average than that of some of the peripheral countries (e.g. Spain, Ireland). Moreover, it would appear that membership of a monetary union accelerates convergence; i.e. if Britain were to join, it could expect its business cycle to move more closely with the core countries. *Per contra*, if Britain remains outside the eurozone, eurozone economies will converge more closely with each other rather than with Britain.

The problems of interest rate convergence and a suitable exchange rate have already been discussed. Suffice it to say that while the exchange rate issue has been a problem in the past - i.e. the pound has been overvalued - today the exchange rate is not a problem. But what of the future? Just as pre-announcement of the convergence rates for the euro in 1997 'steered' participating currencies in the right direction, it is likely that pre-announcement of an entry rate for Britain of (say) €1.37, the PPP rate, would have the desired effect.

In conclusion, it is worth quoting from Begg *et al*, on the crucial question of the opportunity costs of remaining outside the eurozone:

The Sixth Test should be whether the further gains of waiting outweigh the further costs of waiting. Those who argue that the UK can afford to wait until the convergence tests are met 'beyond reasonable doubt' have ignored the first lesson of economics. Optimal behaviour equates the marginal costs and the marginal benefit. Driving the marginal benefit of waiting to zero means waiting too long (p13).

Conclusion

This article has resumed the main economic arguments about the euro. The

---

16. Both sets of figures are from R. Layard, 'The case for joining the euro', LSE Centre for Economic Performance Public Debate, 28.4.03. Trade here means trade in goods (sum of imports and exports).

'costs' of failing to join outweigh the 'benefits' of staying out. As Willem Buiter, David Begg, Richard Layard, Robin Marris and many others have argued, if this is true today, then the longer Britain waits, the greater the opportunity costs incurred. Moreover, only once it is committed to joining can Labour help push for growth-orientated change in eurozone monetary and fiscal policy. Why then have we not joined?

The answer is clearly political - more precisely, it is about political weakness. When the Labour government came to power in 1997, the tabloid press was against the euro and public opinion was divided. Gordon Brown at the Treasury was already sceptical, and Tony Blair was unconvinced that a referendum could be won. The 'doctrine of unripe time' was borne - we would only join when it could be shown to be unambiguously in the country's interests to do so. The pro-euro *Britain In Europe* campaign was put on hold; debate could not begin until the Treasury had ruled, and unless Brown backed euro-entry, the debate could not be won. Blair - whether by design or by default - handed the Treasury and its allies at the Bank of England a veto. Central Banks are generally reluctant to abolish themselves, and no Ministry of Finance wants its powers constrained by treaty obligations, particularly those of Maastricht. Both the Treasury and the BoE had bitter memories of 'Black Wednesday', and suspected the Bundesbank of *schadenfreude*. Moreover, as Brown became stronger at the Treasury and more sceptical on the euro, Blair became less able to shift him to another Cabinet post. Even after the resounding Labour victory in 2001 - which saw the Independence Party lose its deposits - the Government was unable to decide on a referendum. In the post 11 September environment of the 'war on terror', Britain's alliance with the US became ever more visible. By late-2002, word was out that the Treasury assessment would be negative. The more Blair enthused about Britain's key role in Europe, the less believable he became.

Brown's announcement on 9 June and his twitchy press conference with Blair the following day changed almost nothing. True, there will now be a new 'road show' in which the Labour leadership will extol the virtues of Europe. But it is painfully obvious that in the absence of a positive assessment of the five tests by the Chancellor, the road show will peter out just as it did after 1997. As Hugo Young pointed out bitterly, since the 'five tests' were first decreed and the decision effectively placed in the hands of the Treasury, no effort has been made to steer economic policy in a manner which would return a positive verdict. Politically, New Labour has made no attempt to campaign in favour of a social democratic model for Europe, preferring to extol the virtues of US-style 'flexibility' (*Guardian*, 10.6.02).

This is not the first time Britain has been late. It waited 16 years to sign the Treaty of Rome and delayed its decision on joining the EMS until 1992, choosing the worse possible moment. Tellingly, throughout the period Britain has remained locked into its 'special relationship' with the Unites States; in that capacity, first it acted as conduit for the 'Third Way' and 'triangulation' schemes of Clinton, and more recently it has teamed up with the radical right in Washington against the main EU countries.

Perhaps the time has passed and Britain will never join the euro, preferring instead to form a free-trade area with America; this is the preferred solution of Murdoch, Black and right-wing economists like Patrick Minford. Perhaps, as Robin Marris has argued: ' … there will soon be only three significant currencies in the world - the dollar, the euro and an Asian currency based on the yen … If sterling stayed out, our currency would become the repository of large amounts of short-term funds, unwanted at any particular time in the other three … our society and economy would be seriously damaged' (*Guardian*, 1.2.00). Or perhaps even more pessimistically, as John Gray has argued: 'So long as it serves the Blairite agenda, Britain's deeper integration into the EU spells the end of any European project worthy of the name … not only in foreign and defence matters but also in economic and social policy, Britain's goal will be to 'modernise' Europe on an Anglo-American model' (*New Statesman*, 19.5.03). Whatever position the reader may hold on this question, he or she can be certain (to paraphrase Robin Marris) that the ultimate choice will affect Britain's welfare long after Saddam Hussein and Osama bin Laden are forgotten.

Notes from Palestine January 2003

Adah Kay

Adah Kay describes life in the Gaza strip.

Early on Sunday morning Amira rang to say she was going to Gaza. Tom remained in Ramallah; he had to teach on Monday. I jumped out of bed and was off. On Saturday (25.1.03) news broke that the IDF had demolished four bridges linking a village in northern Gaza, Beit Hanun, with its surrounding areas. The official line was that Hamas had launched 10 Kassam rockets from Beit Hanun at the Negev town of Sderot. Some people here think this is in preparation for an Israeli reoccupation of Gaza. During Saturday night tanks and APCs backed up by helicopters had invaded the Zeitun area of Gaza City.

It was dismal and raining as we drove out of Ramallah through the outskirts of Jerusalem and then south west. Weaving between Israel and the Occupied Territories, the contrasts between first and third worlds on these journeys never cease to shock. The weather brightened and more palms appeared in the flatter landscape as we approached Gaza.

We got through the Erez checkpoint, gateway to Gaza and the only part of the occupied territories under Palestinian control, with no hassle. It felt like Checkpoint Charlie, but with no exchange of spies on the long pathway leading between concrete bollards, to the Palestinian side.

Gaza City felt enormous, flat and poor. I kept thinking we were driving through or by camps, but we weren't. We passed kilometres of drab concrete apartment blocks, shack houses crowded together, some with corrugated iron

Notes from Palestine January 2003

fences festooned with bits of rags, wide dirt roads and narrow alleys, very few shops, and, in between, patches of rubbish-strewn wasteland on which goats grazed. Cars and trucks were at least equalled by horse or donkey driven carts sitting low on the road, laden with everything from building materials to vegetables. It felt sombre as most of the shops were shut in mourning for those that had been killed the night before. Reminiscent of the outskirts of Warsaw, the city is laid out in a grid with majestic boulevards in the centre, and the sea beckoning in the distance; a total contrast to Ramallah, which sprawls across hills and valleys. The familiar TV Gaza image, a small formal garden filled with palms, grass and bushes, sat on the island separating the two large lanes of the main street Salah el Din. A virtual oasis for the people.

We stopped off at two human rights organisations and met some of Amira's old friends. A warm welcome but everyone was exhausted after the sleepless night of shelling. 13 Palestinians had been killed and dozens of industrial buildings destroyed or damaged in the hunt for the Hamas weapons workshops. We had arrived too late for the mass funerals, so went immediately to the Zeitun neighbourhood. On the way, we saw at least a dozen demolished buildings, each with crowds of bystanders, all in densely built up areas. Targeting one building would affect those nearby. The churned up road surfaces were marked by the tread of tanks that left a trail of destruction: skewed and broken electricity poles, jagged pieces of metal, shattered glass, lumps of wood and concrete.

The alley outside a partially demolished printing works was full of men and boys; some had started to clear up the debris. The owner, still in shock, took us round the building. Downstairs a large computer lay smashed on its side, hurled from the floor above. The printing press and other new and expensive pieces of equipment were destroyed. Picking our way gingerly over the floor covered in machine parts, rolls of paper, shattered glass and broken furniture, we climbed up a perilous metal spiral staircase to the gallery. This housed the advanced computer graphic equipment. The light wooden panels separating this level from the workshop below hung in shreds. Glass, wood and metal covered the floor, which was strewn with broken computer parts. A drawer thrown on the floor contained samples of their work, a human rights annual report and children's books and discs. This was a workshop that printed scientific, educational and human rights material, not a rocket-making factory. Hundreds of thousands of dollars of equipment had been destroyed overnight.

Upstairs in the apartment of the family who owned the building, we heard about the shelling and explosions that had pounded the neighbourhood for most of the previous night; terrified, no one had slept. Men sat on chairs lining the walls of the living room. A constant stream of family and neighbours came in and out offering condolences for the damage. Shattered glass from the windows blown out by the force of the shelling and explosions glistened on the floors in every room. In the bedrooms mattresses were piled and cupboard doors wrenched off, revealing stacks of neatly folded clothes. The strength of the shelling had caused cracks in walls and damaged bathroom and kitchen fittings.

A group of women and about a dozen children were in the kitchen, the women and teenage girls wearing the 'hijab' (Muslim scarf). We stood in the doorway feeling a sense of intrusion, yet wanting to express our sympathy. The mother holding a child on her knee shouted out her fear and powerless rage. One teenage girl wore the full black face veil down to her neck. Initially it revealed her eyes and mouth, but as her mother talked, she pulled the veil down completely, shutting us out. The same sad picture of family homes violated and people in a state of shock was repeated in the apartments next door.

We visited some other damaged 'rocket workshops', again ordinary local businesses, a manufacturer of spare car parts and a larger metal works. The same trail of damage and senseless destruction was repeated in every place. Shades of Ramallah last March.

In the Sejaya district, a clothes market had been burnt to the ground. Dense and compact, comprising about 60 shops, the market snaked its way off a narrow alley, a bit like Camden Lock in the old days. Some armed Palestinians had been hiding there and were spotted by a helicopter, which fired a rocket, killing them and starting a fire. The acrid smell of burning lingered on the air; blood was spattered on a wall.

On the main Salah el Din Street three buses stood dragged up onto the pavement, one listed to its side, the other two with their backs completely mangled. One bus was rammed into the front of a house. The house next door to it had brightly decorated doors and walls. A child stood in the doorway; men were sitting in a café just two doors up. Apparently the tank had got stuck in the road. To protect themselves from possible attack, the IDF had commandeered the buses to make a barricade.

The next morning we met S at the entrance to Beit Hanun village, on the

Notes from Palestine January 2003

main road to the Erez checkpoint. The village is poor and dusty, with apartment blocks on the outskirts, crowded houses, shacks and narrow alleys further in, surrounded by orange groves and rolling fields. S is one of the lucky few still working - there are no jobs apart from the odd World Bank emergency, job creation schemes or posts with the PA. All previous sources of employment in Israel were abruptly cut off when the current Intifada started in 2000.

The main road into the village was virtually impassable. The Israelis had blocked it off some weeks ago with bulldozers, leaving a deeply rutted road surface. Cars had to slowly edge their way over large mounds of earth. We went to see 3 of the destroyed bridges that had spanned a small riverbed on the way into the village. Two had been very solid structures, one built by the Turks, the other during the British Mandate. S said it had taken the IDF 5 hours of continuous shelling to destroy them on Saturday. The 'Mandate' bridge was now a wide, caved-in concrete slide, a great playground for a group of little boys. The Turkish bridge was completely destroyed. The third 'modern' bridge was impassable for vehicles, reduced to narrow concrete strips revealing the struts below.

On our way through some iron gates leading to the orange groves of one of the village families, we met 4 girls of about 6-8; one was dragging some broken of branches of wood, the other three looked pregnant. Outside the gates, the pregnant three drew out handfuls of oranges from under their jumpers. I was told they were Bedouin. We walked through the peaceful groves passing some large dogs basking in the sun under trees laden with oranges and stopped in front of a large swathe of brown earth, the ground a swirl of tank treads. The IDF tanks that for the past 18 months or so have parked outside the village make regular forays onto the land, destroying whole stretches of orange groves. Facing us beyond the tree line on the hilly horizon we could see the Israeli Negev town, Sderot.

Coffee with S in his quiet backyard chatting under the washing line. As a sideline to supplement his small salary from the Palestinian Authority, he has partially returned 'to the land' and now raises chickens, turkeys and goats to help pay for four children at university abroad. His wife experiments with medicinal herbs in one corner of the patch. We meet his delicious granddaughter, who shyly peeps out from between her mother's legs, one of the few women in Gaza I saw in jeans and leather jacket.

Soundings

As we drove back to Gaza City through the Jabalya refugee camp (over 90,000 people and where the first Intifada started), the 'hierarchy' of poverty slotted into place. Gaza city was beginning to look positively luxurious compared to the relentless miles of dusty unmade roads, stark apartment blocks, narrow alleys, meagre markets and lack of cars.

In the evenings we visited Amira's friends, chatting, joking, discussing 'the situation', political prospects and swapping stories. I spent a lot of time laughing and playing with their children, a great way to practise my pigeon Arabic. The first thing everyone said was 'the situation here now is really bad'. Then they wanted to know about the Israeli elections. The men had a history of political activism and had spent time (one 20 years) in Israeli prisons. They spoke Hebrew and understood Israelis and Israeli society. One evening we visited Haydr Abd-al Shafi - some call him the Palestinian Mandela - who led the Palestinian delegation at Madrid in 1991. We listened spellbound to his tales of that time and his views on the way forward. He is pessimistic in the short term, but convinced that in the longer term only a unity coalition of all political factions (including Hamas and Islamic Jihad) will be able to forge a political strategy and secure a change in leadership.

It was a powerful if brief experience. The contrasts with Ramallah were dramatic. The physical and material environment is harsher, the Islamic influence more visible on the streets, and the different layers of poverty more exposed. Against this backcloth it takes the most extraordinary resilience for people to survive, resist, laugh and hope.

MARX ENGELS COLLECTED WORKS

Volume 49 of this 50 volume series was published in 2002. It contains Engels' correspondence from the late 1880s and early 1890s. The final volume will be published later in 2003. On completion the series will contain all the works of Marx and Engels, whether published during their lifetimes or since.

> 'Indispensable to anyone with a serious interest in Marx, Marxism and the nineteenth century It is unlikely that this edition of the Collected Works will ever need to be replaced.'
> E. J. Hobsbawm

Save 45% on bookshop prices!

Each volume normally costs £ 45.00. For the last year before completion of the series Lawrence and Wishart are running a special mail order offer: Pay now for the complete set and get all 50 volumes for the discounted price of £1250 (plus p&p)

Offer ends on 31 December 2003

Send cheque payable to Lawrence and Wishart Ltd or Visa / MasterCard details (card number, expiry date and your name and address as they appear on your statements) to:

Lawrence and Wishart Ltd, 99A Wallis Rd, London, E9 5LN or e-mail credit card details to orders@l-w-bks.demon.co.uk

Youth groups and the politics of time and space

Nora Räthzel

Nora Räthzel looks at the ways in which a group of marginalised young people seek to make sense of their world.

While writing the first draft of this work, in the summer of 2001, I was haunted by pictures of the violence of the Italian police against those demonstrating in Genoa. The television showed stains of spilled blood on the floors and walls of a hall in which the protesters had been sleeping. Almost a year after the event court proceedings confirmed what the protesters had always claimed: that they had been framed by the police. Policemen had planted the weapons that they then found in the young people's dormitories.

Where would the young people we had interviewed - many of whom had been involved in street violence - stand in such a confrontation today?[1] Would

---

1. This article is based on a three-year research study of young people in a large German town between 1996 and 1999, in parallel to a similar project in London. The majority of the young people were German born, but their parents had been born in 13 countries, including Germany. The Volkswagenstiftung funded the German part of the research and the ESRC the British part. Names of places and people have been changed to protect the anonymity of the respondents

they belong to the police who were celebrating the death of a demonstrator they had shot? Would they be demonstrating in the Pink Block or in the Black Block? Or would they belong to the onlookers shaking their heads in disbelief about this group or the other? I do not know. The young people described here will have by now moved on in some direction. Yet the conditions under which they grew up are still there and experienced by others.

Youth gangs like the one which is the subject of this paper have existed for centuries, and will continue to exist. The image of the spilled blood of protesters provides a good background for understanding their lives. It reminds us not to think of violence as practised only by those positioned at the margins of society, but to see it also as a means used by institutions of the state against those it considers to be the enemies of its reign. Before any of the young people in our sample were born, the violent dimension of state power was already in place. They grew up knowing about it, fearing it or wishing for its protection.

In this article I focus on two particular groups of young people from our study, from the neighbourhood which I call Mixville (the groups were known as the 'Jasons' and the 'Edisons'). The groups were special, in so far as many of the young people in our wider sample, as well as the members of the two groups themselves, saw them as 'gangs'. Though some of the younger people in our sample reported themselves to be members of these 'gangs', most of the interviews I draw on in the following text were conducted with older group members, who were either attending vocational education or had started an apprenticeship.

I will present here a few dimensions of the ways in which members of these two youth groups described their lives in the streets, focusing in particular on their perceptions of time and space. They were in a transitional phase from youth to adulthood, leaving school and entering the labour market, but they were trying to hold on to their traditions and their youthful behaviours and old friendships. I want to explain why this was the case, through looking at the ways in which members of the two groups described themselves, in terms of the places they occupied and the traditions they related to. The stage of transition from adolescence to adulthood is usually seen as a time in which young people fluctuate between different places and time-structures, but it seems to invoke the desire for unchangeable places and circular time structures in these young group members. This article makes an attempt to explain these desires through an analysis of the spatial and political context in which these young people of migrant background live. Positioned as they are as 'foreigners', in a society which rejects them as legitimate members, holding on to a place in which diversity is seen as an asset can seem like the only way to preserve a sense of belonging and self-respect. However, I also argue that such active appropriation of a place can also be seen as reproducing the relegation to a marginal place.

Dangerous places - dangerous people

I want to start with the way in which the two youth groups are talked about by some young people in our sample:

> *Carl* There are always some people standing in front of the school. Recently they have ripped somebody's clothes, they call themselves Jasons, say the teachers.
> *Katrin* I don't have much to do with those Jasons. They are my friends as well, but they're not my cup of tea. They are there for you, if somebody needs to be beaten up or something like that. But they are not my kind of thing. Somehow I am not such a violent person.
> *Ami* Adan Square, that's the ultimate meeting place, there are so many kids hanging around there. I don't know anybody who would ever go there in the evening, except if you know them. For instance, if I knew somebody who knows them, I'd go there.
> *Viky* There are two from Adan Square in our youth centre. I don't like them that much, because they think they can achieve something with violence and I hate that. But these two are quite nice.
> *Hassan* Adan Square, there are a lot there who are into violence and I'm not. I live there so I pass by and sometimes I play there. But they don't do anything.
> *Hamide* On Koray Adan Square you find the Jasons, but you find them also everywhere else, where there is a fight. I find that totally childish, they play the cool ones with their idiotic fights.
> *Interviewer* And what if you come to the square and say, you want to play basketball, would they chase you away?
> *Hamide* No, I don't think so. They'd play with you.

Certainly, the young people on Koray Adan Square are infamous, they are identified with violence. On the other hand, most of those who reject them

Youth groups and the politics of time and space

Koray Adan Square Mixville © *Stefan Schölermann*

have contact with some of them or would like to have some. Other young people do not believe the group is dangerous at all:

> *Clara* People say there are gangs. For example there are the Jasons, the famous ones, who cause a bit of stress sometimes. But I don't think they're really dangerous. It's not as if they kill anybody, or anything.

The Jasons are associated with a certain square in the neighbourhood and often called after it. The same is true for other groups in the area, which are named after the streets and squares on which they spend most of the time: there are the Edisons, from Edison Street, the Kings from Kings Street, and so on. We find this phenomenon described in most writings on youth gangs; the appropriation of places, which are then defended as turfs, is a common feature. The significance of this process in the context of our study lies in the fact that it is specific to the neighbourhood of Mixville, as opposed to the other neighbourhood we studied - which we called Monoville. There, places were also seen as dangerous because they were occupied by dangerous people; however, these people were always named after their ethnic background. A place was described as dangerous because Turks or Russians had occupied it. People were seen as being inherently dangerous and therefore making places dangerous. In Mixville dangerous places and dangerous people signified each other. People were seen as dangerous if and because they had the habit of hanging out in a certain place. This made the relationship between people and places more fluid, because being dangerous was not inscribed into one's ethnicity but rather related to the places one chose to visit regularly.

I have elsewhere discussed the different ways of perceiving violence in Mixville and Monoville, through examining the histories, representations and lived spaces of these two neighbourhoods.[2] Here I will look at the way in which two groups see their group formation and their relation to the places they occupy.

The foundation of a group

> *Aylin* I hang out with the Jasons from Koray Adan Square.
> *Interviewer* And why on that square precisely?
> *Aylin* Because it's so quiet there, we can talk.
> *Interviewer* Quiet? (The interviewer is informed by stories like the ones quoted above.)
> *Aylin* Yes, because everybody comes there, everybody who is in the clique, they live around the square, that's why they hang out there most of the time.

One might have guessed that group members would see themselves differently from the way in which they are seen by others, and the contrast is indeed striking:

> *Zafer* Well, I've known him (pointing at the boy next to him), let's say, for twelve years, him (pointing at someone further away) for five, six years, and it's because we have known each other for a long time. Before, we did not have such cliques; we were too young for that. And then, it just happened that we became a clique of people, because we have known each other so long. When we were together, this was our street, there were our

---

2. 'Living differences: ethnicity and fearless girls in public spaces', in *Social Identities*, Volume 6, No. 2, 2000, pp119-142.

grandmothers, the little ones were there, and the middle ones. We lived closely together and knew each other well, our parents also knew each other. There are not so many new people, that is, people we've gotten to know recently, say during the last year, or the last two years.

The story of the formation of the Edisons is similar:

Necai The group was never founded officially. In the middle of 1995 we met at the playing ground in Bosch Street, and then somebody had the idea that, because we all lived in Edison Street, we should call ourselves the Edison gang. But we have known each other since childhood, really a long time. And everybody knows everybody through school and there we have been able to build even a closer relationship. But since 1995 we are a group, that's how it is.
Interviewer And how long have you been a member?
Necai Me? Since I was born.

In Zafer's account the transition from an extended family to the youth group appears to be a natural process occurring as a result of coming into a specific age. A similar naturalisation is visible in Necai's statement about being a member of the group since he was born. This reference to a common origin determines their future stability: 'Once Edison always Edison', declares Aylin.

These stories are reminiscent of the myths recounting the histories of nation-states. A nation-state that cannot claim an existence of at least one thousand years is not taken seriously, and will not give its dedicated members the sense of a quasi-natural belonging. Only if things will always be the same as they have always been can a sense of security be maintained. It is this desire for something stable, eternal and therefore natural, that these stories speak about. The model after which the groups are shaped is the family: 'We are all brothers and sisters,' says Zafer. 'That's how we see each other. Sometimes there are conflicts, but we are really like a family, everything is being solved.' This construction of the group as a family (or as the ideal of a family) can be understood as constructing biographical time as a continuous, reliable process. Time flows in a circular way, like the seasons in nature. One can count on things repeating themselves periodically. Zafer's story of how his group acquired its name tells us something about his relation to societal time. It talks about a historical continuity that materialised 'behind the back' of its actors:

Zafer The name came really from my big brother. Here in Mixville, it was, it is like, you don't say the name, you say, 'Hi Jason, how are you doing?' My brother was at the fun-fair and there you can have something printed on your jacket in nice letters. So my brother had Jasons written on his jacket. And then he didn't wear the jacket anymore, and I walked around with it. And one day, the Koray Adan people wanted to change their name, because it didn't sound cool anymore, and we wanted a new name, we searched, searched, and then someone said, the colleagues said, we should do what I had done, and then I asked my brother, and then we all discussed it, decided, and that's how the name Jasons came.

And the Jasons, they existed before, about twenty years ago, and the clique was - there weren't so many people, about ten, twenty people, and they used crime, robbery, and all. And then they were grabbed by the police, and they had to dissolve the group, because, they all had a lot of problems. We didn't know that such a group existed as early as twenty years ago, when we started our group. We learned that later from those - what do you call them

Market Place in Mixville © *Stefan Schölermann*

again - yes, those social workers in Spider. They told us that such a thing had already existed and that they thought it was strange, as if we wanted to copy them, but we didn't know that.

It is quite possible that the tradition of greeting each other with 'hi, Jason' marks a trace, a subconscious memory of the older group, which existed not twenty, but ten years before. Zafer tells the story as a way of relating to and distancing his group from that tradition at the same time. 'The Jasons existed before' marks the connection made between the present group and the old one. The insistence that they did not know about the group before they decided on their name allows Zafer to distance his group from the criminal record of the former one, especially in front of the social workers. Yet their story is told in a compassionate tone, to a certain extent from the point of view of the group, or a worried friend, rather than from the point of view of someone condemning their actions. They are described as *having* had a lot of problems. A more critical narrator might have said that they had *caused* a lot of problems. Two histories are constructed in the narrative: first, there is the recent history of the group Zafer belongs to. It shows him and the other group members as active inventors of a name, and

Market Place in Mixville © Stefan Schölermann

therefore of an identity of the group. Although he describes himself as having an important role in the name-giving, he is more interested in representing the process as democratic, everybody has a say. Asking Zafer's brother also indicates that they respect the original 'ownership' of the name. Secondly, this old history of that other, dangerous, group, which they learned about from the social workers, gives their own creativity and inventiveness an additional dignity. They have reinvented (if in a different form) an older tradition of youth gangs in the neighbourhood. When their rival group, the Edisons, retell the story, Zafer's account is reversed and the naming becomes a conscious act of re-naming, of claiming the old group's tradition:

> *Interviewer* I have heard that the other group is also called KAS, the abbreviation for Koray Adan Square?
> *Cemal* Yes, that was earlier, two years ago, when they wrote KAS everywhere, but now they have called themselves Jasons again. The Jasons have been active before, ten, fifteen years ago, that group already existed. They heard about that.

Historical continuity is constructed on two time-dimensions: individual or biographical time (*we have always been friends*) and societal time (*there have always been youth gangs*). By constructing biographical time as continuous, social relations are at once homogenised and frozen, providing a sense of a secure social network. By constructing societal time as a perpetual reproduction of the same, societal relations are naturalised, whatever happens becomes inevitable, any intervention futile:

> *Veli* Yes, one should prevent violence, but how? You can't prevent it. Even if you prevent it today, the little ones, they will certainly do it again, because they become older and older. And then they say, yes, we also want to be like the old ones, one day. Then they'll do it as well.

These images of continuity and reproduction are developed against an experience of the contrary. First, the groups are not as consistent as portrayed by the members. Zafer, who described the Jasons as an extension of his family, had not always belonged to the group:

Interviewer Does that mean you have always been in the clique?
Zafer No, I belonged to another clique. I used to be in my street, in my surroundings, what was closest to me. I was together with my colleagues before, and then we had arguments, and the ones from Koray Adan Square, they were also my friends, so I went to them, as I did not get on with my colleagues any more.

Cemal from the Edisons has made the opposite move:

> I did hang out with the Jasons for a while, but I realised that they were not, how should I put it, well, they were not the right friends for me. We are very different from them.

Katrin, who says she grew up with the Edisons and hangs around with them, distances herself from the Jasons because she thinks they are too violent. But it is precisely this violence she takes advantage of, when somebody 'needs to be beaten up', as she puts it. Second, not only do members drift from one group into another one, the relations between groups vary as well. For instance, the Edisons describe the Jasons as wanting to be the coolest by doing the most stupid things (an expression to describe violence and petty theft), while they themselves are basically the good ones. At the same time they describe each other as friends who share places like youth centres and help each other against groups from other neighbourhoods. Third, though they represent their groups as everlasting communities, they know that their future is doomed:

> *Zafer* Really, don't know, it was different before. Before, we did everything together, we went everywhere, we did everything together; no matter if it was fighting, going to the movies, to a disco, we did everything together. It is not like that any more, because we have grown older and everyone has their private life now. I am working, the colleague here (pointing at his neighbour) is still in school, and he (pointing at another boy) is doing a preparatory year. Everybody is different, nobody finds the time anymore, to be all together again, like a family. There is only ever five, six, people, who go to the disco, or so. We used to do everything together, *everybody goes their own way now.*
> *Necai* We have seen that the Edisons, everybody took care of everybody else.

It was like that, only now, one has an apprenticeship, the other is getting married soon, this and that, and *everybody goes their own way*. But everywhere, where we meet, or we know where to find someone, if we need him, we know the place.

Zafer's continuous repetition of the phrase 'we did everything together' indicates his deep worry about the changes that have occurred. It is as if repeating the sentence again and again could bring back those times. Necai's account is more hopeful - he still believes that in spite of their different trajectories the Edisons will still be able to find and support each other. Both accounts include the expression *everybody goes their own way* - signifying spatial movement as well as a process; this would be called individualisation in theories of modernisation or of a 'reflexive modernity'. However, to understand the character of this process the concept of *privatisation* seems more adequate. Privatisation is commonly used to describe a transition of bodies from public into private ownership. The etymology of the word leads to the Latin word 'privare', which means, 'to deprive (this word retains the Latin root), rob, free'. The private man, seen as the free man, is at the same time the man deprived of his social relations.[3] When Zafer says that everybody has a private life now and therefore many do not come to the group any more, he points at this process of deprivation. The young people moving on to jobs and into families lose connection with their former friends and are thus deprived of the common ground that enabled them to support each other. If each one goes his/her own way, their experiences will differ. Following one's own way includes the absence of other marchers on that path and this excludes the possibility of finding support. Becoming a worker also means that individuals are positioned against each other as competitors for jobs.

The two boys telling these stories are both seventeen years old. Zafer attends a course that is supposed to prepare him for an apprenticeship, while Necai attends a vocational school to become an office worker. They have left the place where most of their friendships were formed, at school. Yet they do not want to, or are not able to, let go of their old lives. They still frequent the same places they gathered at when they went to school together. At the same time

---

3. I use the male form deliberately, since the construction of the free private man excludes women.

they are aware that not only have their friends changed and started to disappear, the places themselves have changed as well:

> Cemal A lot of Yugoslavs have come here over the last year, and gypsies and so on, who have been begging in the streets. Of course, that doesn't fit into our neighbourhood, to say it bluntly. But, it used not to be that way in the past and I really don't want to accept changes. I want Mixville to stay as it always is, that we always stay friends and can hang out together every day. But we can't do it every day.

For Cemal Mixville 'as it always is' (the use of the present tense where the past tense would be appropriate signifies the desire to freeze the present state) is synonymous with the place where friends always stay friends. Like his peers with German background, this young man of Turkish descent ascribes threatening changes in the neighbourhood to foreigners. His desire for stability is tainted by the knowledge that this stability is doomed, in fact has already vanished. The only way to preserve it is to dwell in the past; therefore Cemal wants to become a writer: 'Later I want to get an education and I would like to become a writer and write a book about us, about the Edison gang, the way we were in the past. I think the book will become a big success.'

Necai wants to reshape the past by constructing a different present for people in the future to remember: 'We, that is our street, we were worse before, our older people, our brothers, they were worse. We try to build a generation where there is a youth gang of which one used to say ... well, they thought for a while that we did only stupid things. We have tried to produce justice, but differently, not through discussion, but through violence, so people would understand us. But now, we want to be like ... that later, people will say about us that we were good, not bad.' Necai wants to break the tradition of the violent youth gang, to reinvent it through a new presence that will become the group's identity for the future. His aim for continuing the group is therefore also to change it.

That the young people we spoke to hold on to a past that is rapidly changing suggests that it fulfils a need for them that cannot be fulfilled by other means. Wanting to have friends on whom one can rely in times of need seems reasonable enough. But why do they have to form a group? The first answer which can also be found in literature on youth gangs, was given above: Zafer mentioned how the

Edisons help the Jasons when groups from outside the neighbourhood attack them, and Katrin says: 'yes, that's the way it is today, young people are that way, they look for trouble, and if you are not in a clique today, you are really lost.' This may explain why young people choose to be in youth groups while they are at school and can become the victims of other people their age. However, it does not explain why some of them want to hold on to their group when this threat has vanished because the threatening groups have dissolved. An explanation can be found in Zafer's and Veli's description of their daily lives in the street:

> *Veli* We stay on the streets, because after 6 p.m. that's when the day really starts to begin for us again, and then it's cold and we decide, say, to go to the Mall, with five, six, people, and when we are sitting at a corner there, the guards come and chase us out, because we …
> *Zafer* Yes, and then it's like 'the Turks' again, or …
> *Veli* Because we stick out.
> *Zafer* Because we're foreigners.
> *Veli* And then they ban us from the place.
> *Zafer* Just because of the way we look, they don't let us in. It's like: 'I don't like your face, get out of here.' For instance there is that bin, where you can put out your fags. Somebody, a German guy, smokes and nobody says anything. A colleague goes there, and it's like: 'Come on, put out your cigarette and get out. You're banned for today!' 'Why?' 'You're not allowed to smoke here.' And I say, 'but there was just somebody smoking.' 'That's not true, I am sorry, you have to get out.' It's not as if it happens all the time, but it happens.
> *Interviewer* Have you done anything to change it?
> *Zafer* We can't do anything because we'll always have the poor hand. If we don't do anything, we're back on the street. If we do something, then the police will be there in a minute: 'Oh yes, we know you, you've been here before, come with me.'
> *Veli* We have no chance. We just want to be left alone. When we show up, they think we want to turn the whole place upside down. We're constantly observed. They're afraid of young people. They think we are all the same.
> *Zafer* They have no idea how we really are. They cannot say we're all the same, they can't say we're all assholes; they can't say we're all good.

Mixville Street © Stefan Schölermann

The way in which the two boys pick up each other's sentence and continue them transmits the sense of a story that has been experienced and told many times. There are different ways of interpreting this passage. As the boys expect the police to take them away, because they know them to disturb the order, the passage can be read as a form of self-victimization, a way of seeking pity from the interviewer and from adults in general. At the same time we know from the wider literature, and from numerous accounts, that black and migrant youth are subject to more surveillance, and stopped more often by the police, than their white and non-migrant peers. No matter whether or not the boys here have contributed to the way they are perceived, what counts for them is that they are treated as suspicious irrespective of what they do. As the guards cannot possibly know whether they are good or not, it would not make any difference if they were. They would still face the same problems; they would still have no place to go where they would be accepted.

By contrast, two girls in our study with German background told us how they used the Mall. They went to the roof and observed the people using the sauna in the neighbouring building. It was forbidden to go to the roof and the girls were thrown out sometimes. But for them this was a sport. They tried to see how long and how often they could stay without being found. No matter how often they were thrown out, they were never banned.

For the guards and for the police, the non-native boys, especially those with a Turkish background, are the ones who occupy the subject position of the troublemakers in Mixville. Therefore, the trouble caused by boys and girls with a German background is perceived as the normal nonsense young people their age are bound to do. The same behaviour coming from young people with a migrant background evokes images of dangerous youth who must be stopped from the outset. Even when German boys become members of a youth group considered as a gang, they are not seen as occupying the same position as the migrant boys and girls within that group. One social worker, who was keen to dissolve the Edison group in order to transform them into decent boys, had only a dismissive remark for German boys joining gangs: 'They probably only do it because they are afraid of the gangs'. While this could be the case for some boys, as a statement about German boys in general it assumes that there is an inherent difference between young migrants forming or joining groups and young native Germans doing so.

Unchanging places, cyclic time and the question of marginalisation

We can now begin to make a connection between the everyday life of these groups of young people and their desire for the security that unchanging places and circular time provide. I would like to suggest that this desire to hold on to a naturalised peer group and to an unchanging place, as well as the belief that time keeps repeating itself, is engendered by experiences of marginalisation and discrimination. By going into the shopping mall they make the transition from the public streets of their neighbourhoods to the private space of the mall. On a local level they transcend the appropriated space of their childhood to step into the privatised space of capital, the space that awaits them when they begin working. In that sense, the behaviour of the guards and the police is a symbol for what they can expect once they leave their neighbourhood and they know this:

Necai Well, we are satisfied with Mixville, happy ... In Mixville I know, if I look backwards somebody else is going to give me cover, somebody will take care of me, but when I am outside Mixville, I know I am totally alone and I get anxious and nervous.

One of the things Necai is afraid of when he leaves Mixville is being attacked by skinheads, as once happened to him and his friend while riding the metro. This anxiety is augmented by his fear of the police. He did not report that attack to the police because he does not want to have anything to do with these authorities. Cemal describes the security that Mixville provides in opposition to the rest of the city:

We are lucky living in Mixville, because outside, in the city, there are a lot more Germans, and there are a lot more people who dislike foreigners, but here in Mixville, most of the Turks and foreigners live here.

As the young men feel that they do not have any place outside Mixville, it is difficult for them to shift their local belonging to a more general level of national or class belonging. Likewise, to belong to one of the lifestyle-groups, which, as some recent theories about youth suggest, have replaced class and national belonging, also seems impossible. This is not because they do not belong to such groups. With their preference for name brand clothes and hip hop they certainly form part of a particular lifestyle. Equally, their parents' social position and their own work aspirations make them members of specific strata of the working class. However, no matter how much they fit into any of these social groups, first and foremost they will be seen as 'foreigners' and treated accordingly.

In Mixville they have been able to create a place they can consider their own, a place that belongs to them and where they belong. They believe (and they may be right) that they have created this place partly through the use of violence. They have not experienced serious racial harassment, they say, 'because in Mixville everybody is afraid of us.' In addition, Mixville provides a home for them because it is a place that accommodates difference. Zafer formulates that well:

If you look at those chains of shops, the Turk starts there, and there the Albanian ends. And where the Albanian ends, the Yugoslav starts with his shop. And I mean, living together here, if we would look at Greece or Turkey ... and here, where the Turks end, you see Greeks and they are fully satisfied with it. I am also learning Greek.

The diverse ethnicities which comprise their groups are seen as an asset, enabling the young people to learn from each other:

Necai Colleagues of mine, a German and a Yugoslav, they came every day and they decided to learn Turkish. I thought that's impossible, but when you hear them now, you'd say that is not a German, not a Yugoslav, his Turkish is perfect ... And if a Yugoslav takes me to his parties and I can learn something about his culture, I think that's great. As long as he accepts me, I can accept him.

In Mixville, diversity, being a 'foreigner', can be seen as the norm. The young people know that this is exceptional for the city they live in, and differs from Germany as a whole. The moment each of them follows their own way, the security they have found in being part of an accepted diversity is lost. It will be difficult for them to recreate similar relations of belonging in other places, which are not structured by diversity in the same way. Therefore, they cannot (or only with great difficulty) accompany the process of privatisation, of being deprived of social relations structured through mutual trust and respect, by a process of individualisation, of becoming unique and independent individuals. Most discussions about the ever-increasing individualisation in postmodernity or late modernity do not take into account that there are people to whom individualisation (in the sense of becoming independent and unique) is denied. The young people presented here are perceived not as individuals in their own right, but as representatives of a type. They are already known and judged before they act. It is not too much individualisation that is their problem, but the impossibility to individualise. 'They think we're all the same,' Zafer said.

In Mixville they are able to counter this portrayal of themselves. Being members of youth groups provides them with a sense of commonality, of sameness in relation to the members of their own group; but at the same time it also gives them a sense of being unique. They differ from other groups in terms of the squares or streets they occupy, and the activities they engage in. These activities enable them to develop their self-esteem by protecting themselves from being put down. As Zafer and Cemal remark: 'Normally we are not harassed that much in the streets, 'cause if people see there are five or six Turks, they think immediately, better not to say anything, they are going to slap us in the face.' It seems difficult to convince young people of the virtues of non-violent behaviour, when they experience that it is precisely the image of being violent that earns them respect, or at least protects them against racist behaviour. That there is some truth in their judgement of the situation may be assumed by the fact that girls of migrant background (in and outside of youth groups) reported a number of incidents where they have been called names and harassed in the streets.

In his lectures on Shakespeare Auden, in analysing Iago, who acts evil just for the fun of it, suggests that the only way for a man to be free is to reject necessity: '... his ego seeks constantly to assert its autonomy by doing something of which the requiredness is not given, something which is completely arbitrary, a pure act of choice'. Such an act can be defined as an *acte gratuit*, like that of an artist, of players who make their own rules or of a criminal: '... a man asserts his freedom by disobeying a law and retains a sense of self-importance because the law he has disobeyed is an important one, one established either by God or society'.[4]

The boys in the groups presented here certainly feel that they live by their own rules and show a desire for a life of self-determination. Necai gives a vivid account of this desire:

> Once, in 1996, I tried to get a room for us. I wrote a letter to the youth office, which I did not mail, but still I got an appointment with a youth worker. The point was, we were always sitting on that playground, and many people complained about us and we were fed up with that, and therefore I wanted to apply for a room, for after the time when the *Workshop* is open, until ten p.m. or so. A room where we are all alone, where everybody can do what they want, but has to clean up everything afterwards. We wanted to organise a disco ourselves, but everything went down the drain, because nobody was interested in us. The room was not supposed to be just for the Edison clique, it should be a youth centre for everybody. We wanted to act as social workers ourselves, and we wanted to do everything they do in a youth centre, but just

---

4. *Lectures on Shakespeare*, Faber, London 2000, p198.

without anybody telling us what to do. And they told us, yes, yes, but in the end nothing came of it. And therefore, I want to especially thank you [directed towards the interviewer] for coming here, for seeking contact with us, for showing an interest in who we are. Because many of us see that as an opportunity to talk, to really say what we think.

Who knows, a self-organised youth centre might not have been viable. It might have ended in destroyed furniture and violent fights between different groups claiming access. Nevertheless, it would have been worth trying, especially as violence and destruction occur in official centres as well.[5] What is important here is that Necai's efforts resulted in confirmation of his and his friends' conviction that nobody trusts them and that nobody cares about them. His story is marked by a contradiction. On the one hand it speaks of a strong desire for independence and self-determination; on the other it is a plea for care, for having people take an interest in them. A similar desire was articulated by Zafer and Veli, when the interviewer asked them how they would like to be treated:

Zafer They should take care of us.
Veli They should not see us as foreigners but as human beings, as people.
Zafer Like any other normal human being, any normal one.

Wanting to be normal provides another clue to the group's sometimes violent actions, and their thefts of brand-name clothes. These could be interpreted as attempts to become just the sort of young people society wants them to be - oriented towards upward mobility, following the latest fashion to satisfy the brand's need for profits. These young people are, in a way, tragic heroes. The more they try to become normal through the only resources they have, the more they are bound to resemble the picture they want to escape - a bunch of dangerous foreigners.

---

5. In his 1961 study *Street Corner Society* (University of Chicago Press), William Whyte reported on a youth centre mainly managed by a former street corner boy of the neighbourhood, which was the only one of three opened at the same time which was successful. In spite of this, it was closed down and the young people that had attended it were back on the streets. It would be interesting to investigate why, with all the concern there is about getting young people off the streets, and preventing criminality, possibilities that do not imply control are rarely tried.

There are a number of theories accounting for the formation and behaviour of youth gangs. Some suggest that young people become delinquent because they learn criminal behaviour from adults; others argue that it is because there is a gap between the expectations society produces and the resources available to realise them; or because these young men lack appropriate male role-models at home; or because they reject middle-class values and acquire working-class values instead, which, it is argued, include a certain kind of masculinity, marked by 'toughness' and 'smartness'. The youth groups in our study tell an additional story. The values they learn do not differ decisively from the middle-class norms they are taught in school. What is different is the way in which these norms are applied to them. If they experience discrimination by the same authorities that represent the values they are asked to follow, how are they supposed to take them seriously? If they are reduced to their ethnic background, and can only find respect through being feared, how are they supposed to believe in the values of equality based on a universal humanity? As Paul Willis once wrote about a similar group of lads, it is not a lack of knowledge that drives young people to become what they are seen to be; it is their insight (however partial) into the ways in which society works to exclude them that motivates their actions.[6] Through their experiences they are bound to transgress the surface of respectable values, and find themselves amidst the machinery of an unjust society. One way of surviving is to play according to the rules that are at work, instead of believing in those that they are taught.

Appropriation of space or appropriated by space? The dialectics of agency and subordination

As Zygmunt Bauman has argued, those who are able to take advantage of postmodern times exist in different modes of space and time from those who are not able to do so:

> For the first world, the world of the globally mobile, space has lost its constraining quality and is easily traversed in both its 'real' and 'virtual' renditions. For the second world, the world of the 'locally tied', of those barred from moving and thus bound to bear passively whatever change may

---

6. In *Learning to Labour. How Working Class Kids get Working Class Jobs*, Saxon House 1977, p126 onwards.

be visited on the locality they are tied to, real space is fast closing up ... People marooned in the opposite world are crushed under the burden of abundant, redundant and useless time they have nothing to fill with. In their time 'nothing ever happens'. They do not 'control' time - but neither are they controlled by it, unlike their clocking-in, clocking-out ancestors, subject to the faceless rhythm of factory time. They can only kill time, as they are slowly killed by it.[7]

The young people in our sample seem to fit perfectly into this description. Their space certainly closes up, and they have an abundance of time:

Zafer We don't really do much, we smoke, everyone talks about their problems, we talk a lot among us, we do things, we make plans, but if an important person can't come, we leave it or we do it all the same. We just pass the time.

Yet, on another level, they do make an effort to control time (if not the actual daily hours); they try to fix and contain it in their stories about everlasting friendships and the circular reproduction of events. They do not 'bear passively' what happens to their local space. They have actively appropriated places and are engaged in a number of activities in order to preserve them. Ironically, it is at the moment of transition, the moment they are meant to go beyond the borders that have surrounded their adolescent lives, that their actions freeze and turn against them. The places they have appropriated seem to have taken hold of them. What was their strength, to root themselves in their neighbourhood, turns into their weakness once the conditions for this kind of rooting begin to disappear. In retrospect, it may seem as if, instead of appropriating places, they have been appropriated by them, reproducing the spatial marginalisation society had designated for them. The place that belongs to them and to which they belong is the place to which they are relegated by the exclusionary practices of society at large.

However, their story does not end here; there remains the other side of the coin. In appropriating these spaces, the young people have also developed their

---

7. In *Globalization. The Human Consequences*, Polity Press, London 1998, p88.

creativity, their social skills and their capacity for solidarity. Even if Necai's attempt to set up an independent youth centre failed, it has provided him and his friends with knowledge about state institutions. The ideas and insights formulated by Necai, Zafer, Veli and Cemal show them clinging to their old ways but also expressing hopes and plans for the future. With the resources they have acquired in shaping their local places, and in being shaped by the possibilities its diversity has to offer, they might eventually be able to move on and recreate new, flexible places of belonging.

I would like to thank Gabriela Mischkowski, Yael Feiler and Angelika Magiros for reading an earlier draft and making very useful comments in spite of their own busy schedules. Many thanks also to Charlotte Nyman for correcting my English

Five poems

Night light

Every evening I don't cook for you
a light bulb lays a goose egg
in a stainless steel spoon, hanging
like a ladled false moon
next to the fish slice and palette knife
behind which angel fish swim
in a white-out, day and night,
on the barred kitchen tiles, getting
nowhere.

So I wait for your call

and the white bulb comes
and goes, growing
strong in the dark.

Lorna Dowell

How to learn to ride a Bicycle

Find a quiet spot without distractions
Every little stone may prove an obstacle.
Ask a friend to help by holding the bicycle.
Sit on the seat and turn the pedals
with both your feet. The idea is
to keep your balance.

Don't look down at your feet, face forward.
Your friend will keep up with you.
Remember it is not as simple as it may look.
You will wobble, he will try to steady you.
Don't blame him if you fall, everybody does,
sooner or later.

It is easier than you think.
It is much harder than you think.
You depend on your friend, but don't
depend on him. Just bear in mind
it is his gift to you. If he has had enough
let him go.

Alice Beer

The pulse

If the heart is a house my parents
live there separated by a wall.

Tall rooms are secretly linked
by long muscular stairs, a pyramid

of light I travel up to the point
of their joining. If only I could see

under their door the glowing bubble
the light comes from, the quick pulse

at the centre beating like concussion:
the hidden verb of their talk.

In a lit corner of the hall
I can see their two bodies bend

apart like a river forking.
Hear their neat footsteps pause

on the turning-point of the stairs.
An exact door clicks.

Then the dark house makes
untranslated language in the night:

pound and pound, pound,
overheard from my bed.

Martha Kapos

Edward Thomas at Arras 1917

Those last years you spent
naming all the things that lay
between the battle-lines.
You noted the first skylark, aspens
about to bud and wrote,
in a last letter to your son
of the ordinary miracle of a working farm
in no-man's land -
a grove of trees, a farm-worker
drawing water from a pump
magnified by your field glasses,
so near, you said: *I could have reached
out and touched it with my hand*,
but that night you woke to the roar
of field-guns, and by dawn light
you looked again and saw
a crater where the farmhouse had stood,
the trees had simply blown away,
and where the dear solid people
had walked - nothing, torn air.

Patrick Early

The entry in Thomas's diary is dated the day before he was killed.

Fountain
for Mike Gleeson

At three years old my father lifted me,
seated me high on cushions,
a little emperor at his desk.

Leaning over, he parted my thumb
and apprentice fingers, closed them
round the fountain of his pen,

its gold nib wet and stained by language,
the inlaid mother-of-pearl
a mystery, silken as his bedside stories.

He led me then across the paper,
my hand hidden in his,
tracing the unformed shape of my name;

dark blue ink rising in the spires
of consonants, stumbling and rolling
into the slopes, the curves of the vowels;

a blue line dividing the sky of my page -
the horizon's promise, a prayer,
the hills toward which I would always be travelling.

Patrick Hobbs

Veil of influence

The legacy of John Rawls
Michael Saward

Michael Saward looks at the influence of the work of John Rawls.

I never met the Harvard political philosopher John Rawls, who died in November 2002, at the age of 81. But as someone teaching and writing about political theory over the past few years I am, like hundreds of others, exploring terrain which he did more to shape than any other theorist of the past century or more. His influence is not always easy to trace; political theory in 2003 is an umbrella term for highly diverse debates, from globalisation to multiculturalism to nationalism, and Rawls's influence is evident in the rejection as much as in the embrace of his style and framework. However, few would begrudge his singular reputation. His masterpiece, A *Theory of Justice* (1971), is a monumental work of grand theory, offering a vision of the just society that is pursued in relentless depth. Its sheer scope, ambition and attention to detail set it apart from English-language political theory as it had been practised for many years previously, among liberals at least.

The importance and influence of Rawls's work is much debated. Rawls did little to promote his ideas; by all accounts he was a reserved and modest man, preferring the quiet life of a philosophy scholar to public or policy advocacy. Though he recast political theory, his critics are legion, from the right and the left, feminists and 'communitarians' and multiculturalists. It is often said that he had much more influence on political theory than on parties and public policy - less influence in the real political world, in other words. But here too the picture is uneven. His legacy, for the liberal left in particular, may come to rest more in the evocative symbols he bequeaths than in particular policy prescriptions. That may sound dismissive, but the symbolic power and attraction of his vision of society as a system of social co-operation among equals may yet prove a counterweight to the micro-managed and marketised world of New Labour.

Breaking the mould?

To assess his legacy, we need to appreciate just how dramatically Rawls changed the contours of political theory. Normative theories that address the legitimacy of state power and action - the big 'ought' questions of politics, and not just the descriptive 'is' ones - were in crisis before A *Theory of Justice*. Prominent figures lamented in the late 1950s and early 1960s that large-scale political philosophy was 'dead'. Others celebrated this apparent demise; the heirs of the 'ordinary language' school were bemused by the idea of grand system-building and sought to concentrate on exploring the common uses and meanings of terms like justice, equality, freedom and rights.

A *Theory of Justice* challenged head-on these claims and suspicions. Rawls criticised 'intuitionism', the idea that we can figure out what (e.g.) equality means by interrogating our intuitive thoughts about it in enough depth. Less directly he challenged Marxist claims that markets wholly undermine equality. Most clearly, however, Rawls attacked his main liberal opponents, the utilitarians, for not taking rights seriously. According to Rawls, utilitarians would be happy with an overall increase in utility or happiness in society, even if its distribution was terribly uneven and many people could not share in it (or worse, were exploited to produce greater utility for others). He argued that: 'In a just society the rights secured by justice are not subject to political bargaining or to the calculus of social interests' (A *Theory of Justice*, p4 - hereafter referred to as *TJ*). In other words, governments and citizens were constrained by rights that must be respected even if ignoring them were beneficial in other ways. Or as the philosophers put it, the right has priority over the good.

At the core of Rawls's theory were the two principles of justice:

(1) each person is to have the equal right to the most extensive liberty compatible with a similar liberty for others
(2) Social and economic inequalities are to be arranged so that they are both (a) to the greatest benefit of the least advantaged; and (b) attached to positions and offices open to all under conditions of fair equality of opportunity.

Veil of influence

This looks complex, but at one level it is not. The first principle holds that we should be free as possible to set the course of our own lives. Rawls is, after all, a liberal. The bottom line was about individual people and their freedom to live their lives as they choose. There was no higher value than liberty.

The intensely debated key part of the second principle is the need to make inequalities work to the benefit of the least advantaged (or the 'worst off'). This is Rawls's famous 'difference principle'. The core idea is this: social and economic inequalities are not wrong, or bad, in themselves. They only become indefensible when they don't operate to improve the position of the worst-off (such as those on the lowest incomes). In the economics-driven jargon, we have to 'maximin' - maximise the minimum payoff. Rawls views society as a large-scale experiment in social co-operation. The luck and the talents of the better off - including their genetic talents, which are just a matter of chance and are not exactly 'deserved' - *can* be used to improve their own wealth and position. If this were not allowed, if we were to take a more radical, levelling egalitarian approach, then according to Rawls individuals would have few incentives to innovate, to create wealth. But, he argued, this is only acceptable up to a point. As long as those in the worst-off positions are benefiting *as well*, then inequalities can be just.

Having principles is fine, of course, but why should we accept *these* ones? Rawls was in no doubt that we all would and should accept them. The two principles do not just come out of the blue. Rawls argues that these would be chosen in an *original position* behind a *veil of ignorance*. The original position is more-or-less Rawls's version of the much older 'state of nature' of famous contract theorists like Hobbes, Locke and Rousseau. It is an imaginary place, an 'initial position', outside society, where a group of people meet, in order to define 'the fundamental terms of their association' - or, how their society should be shaped and run. People in the original position are behind a veil of ignorance: they don't know their age, class, race, religion, or any other particular facts about themselves. They are choosing, self-interested people, but stripped down to their human essence. In this odd, hypothetical position, behind the veil, Rawls asks: what principles would they (you, me) choose to govern the basic structure of society?

The trick behind the original position and the veil of ignorance is that, because we are stripped of our particular identities, we are forced to choose for everyone (or - for anyone we *might* be). Self-interest is made to work for the common good. By using the original position and the veil, writes Rawls, 'One excludes the knowledge of those contingencies which sets men at odds and allows them to be guided by their prejudices' (*TJ*, p19). The circumstances of the choosing make the ultimate choices - for his two principles - fair and impartial. Rawls assumes that these rational people (that is, all of us) would prioritise freedom of speech, expression, worship, and so on (the first principle), but that we would also want to guard against our being at the bottom of the social and economic heap by making sure the rich can only get richer if the poor also benefit in the process.

That is the gist of his theory of justice. The theory has generated so much debate that thousands of articles have been written subjecting every small element in this argument to forensic examination. But the big picture is this: in 1971, this was a tremendously and unusually ambitious attempt to get to the root of what justice means and why we should accept a just society along these lines. Referring to Rawls's revival of the idea that 'a person has a dignity and worth that social structures should not be permitted to violate', Chicago philosopher Martha Nussbaum writes that: 'Thirty years after publication of *A Theory of Justice*, with all the discussion of rights and pluralism that has ensued, it is easy to forget that a whole generation of our political and moral philosophers had virtually stopped talking about that idea, and about how it can guide a religiously and ethnically diverse society like our own'.[1]

I have concentrated so far on *A Theory of Justice*, but Rawls has published other books since then, most notably *Political Liberalism* (Columbia University Press, 1993). In this book, Rawls defends his theory of justice as 'political not metaphysical'. He moves to a view where people in a society may have 'comprehensive doctrines', such as religious convictions, which are incompatible with others' similar doctrines. But still we have to live together. So placing limits on how people reason *in public* is important - they should not argue from within their comprehensive doctrines, but rather offer arguments that others can reasonably agree with. In that way, one might be able to achieve an 'overlapping consensus' among adherents to different comprehensive doctrines.

---

1. M. Nussbaum, 'The Enduring Significance of John Rawls', *The Chronicle of Higher Education*, 20.7.01.

Political Liberalism seemed to be different to *A Theory of Justice* - more political, grounded, realistic, accepting pluralism of faith and belief more fully. It put the original position to one side, as just one way among legitimate others of finding one's way into public reason, and seemed less ambitious, addressed as it was only to those already living in liberal democratic societies. Certainly some liberal political theorists were dismayed. Brian Barry, reviewing *Political Liberalism*, wrote: 'I believe that the first time Rawls got it roughly right, and that the line he pursues in the new book is thoroughly misguided' (*Guardian*, 14.8.93). My own view is that, despite surface appearances, little really changed in Rawls's theory from the first to the second book, and that critics who assumed otherwise were paying too much attention to changes in wording and not enough to deeper continuities of structure. For example, debate in the 'public political forum' in *Political Liberalism* seems different from the original position of the earlier book, but individuals are similarly restricted in the type of arguments that can be put forward to others.[2]

Influence and importance

The influence of *A Theory of Justice* on political ideas has been uneven. Anglo-American liberal political philosophy was reshaped by it - Rawls's book set the parameters for debate from the moment it was published. Prominent philosophers in that tradition have been fulsome in their tributes to Rawls; Thomas Scanlon of Harvard says that Rawls's work 'revived and reshaped the entire field, and its profound influence on the way justice is understood and argued about will last long into the future'. Joshua Cohen of MIT says that Rawls 'wouldn't have gone in for rankings, but his work has a place among the greatest tradition of moral and political philosophy that would include Plato, Aristotle, Rousseau'.[3]

In the political world itself, Rawls's influence is more uncertain, and difficult to detect. His brand of 'left-wing liberalism' may have seemed radically welfarist in the US, but much of continental Europe, with established collectivist traditions and widely-accepted welfare state provision, could view his ideas as rather mainstream. There is little evidence of direct influence on US Supreme

---

2. See M. Saward, 'Rawls and Deliberative Democracy', in M. Passerin d'Entreves (ed.), *Democracy as Public Deliberation*, Manchester University Press 2002.
3. 'Rawls Remembered', *The Philosophy Magazine*, Issue 22, 2003, p34.

Court decisions or on Democratic Party ideology or policy - especially into the Clinton era. In the UK, the establishment of the Social Democratic Party in the early 1980s led to a flurry of interest in Rawls's ideas; former Labour deputy leader Roy Hattersley has been most prominent in discussing Rawls in mainstream UK politics, and claiming for him a place at the centre of Labour thinking. Beyond this, A *Theory of Justice* has been translated into more than 25 languages, and it has been said to have been influential among some Chinese dissident groups. That should be no surprise. As Rawls argued, 'The limitation of liberty is justified only when it is necessary for liberty itself' (*TJ*, p28).

The critics

Even Rawls's admirers are his critics. The libertarian right were upset by his difference principle apparently forcing the better off to work for others without their consent - a sort of inverse wage slavery. Feminists have criticised the way in which he has apparently taken the institution of the family as natural, overlooking injustices that can arise for individuals within families. More recently, critics who stress the importance of recognising social and cultural difference wonder, on a philosophical level, if the 'person' in the original position is really a person at all, so stripped are they of all the particularities that make them who they are in the first place. Communitarians criticise the abstract individualism of Rawls's theory, arguing that we draw our sense of self from the localities and communities we inhabit, and that we possess no 'essence' beyond that.

On the left there is a good deal of argument about just how egalitarian Rawls's theory is. Clearly the difference principle supports a quite extensive welfare state funded through general taxation and designed to operate to the benefit of those in the most vulnerable socio-economic positions. At the same time, the acceptance of some inequalities, along with the priority accorded to individual liberty and the clear acceptance of the market society, made many on the left suspicious. This ambiguity led to his use by both sides in debates from the 1980s over the 'crisis of the welfare state' across Europe. As Cecile Laborde has written, 'Rawls's emphasis on the priority of liberty and on the acceptability of inequality provided ammunition to those "neo-liberals" arguing for welfare cuts and market-based policies ... while his rehabilitation of distributive justice, by contrast, was attractive to those within the post-Marxist or non-Marxist left who sought to reconcile egalitarianism with economic liberalism'.[4] But the Blairite left (or perhaps 'right'), along with Clinton Democrats and many other European social democratic parties, have different agendas to that of Rawls. As Ben Rogers has written, left-of-centre parties and governments across the west 'speak the language of community, not of individual rights; of equality of opportunity, rather than equality of outcome; of desert rather than the difference principle' (*Prospect*, June 1999, p55).

A legacy for the left?

The sheer scope and richness of Rawls's work will no doubt secure its future influence. As with other classics of political theory, it will prove to be a source of insight and inspiration for new political concerns and challenges. For example, one of the basic arguments of A *Theory of Justice* is that we do not *deserve* our genetic inheritance; it's just a matter of chance. Therefore, we do not have a right to benefit from exploiting our genetic advantages. Maybe it is reasonable, even desirable, to manipulate the genetic make-up of unborn babies? This is not an argument Rawls anticipated, but we are now making decisions about the uses of relevant technologies. Being very selective and speaking from a broadly left-liberal perspective, I would single out three broader areas where Rawls might continue to be influential, in no particular order.

First, although it has been sidelined in more recent work, by Rawls as well as by his commentators, the original position continues to offer a beguiling image of an ideal decision-making procedure, embodying openness, equality, impartiality and inclusiveness. Could it be approximated in the real political world? The past ten years or so have seen a highly fruitful debate about 'deliberative democracy' - indeed Rawls declared himself a deliberative democrat in the late 1990s.[5] Part of that debate was about potential decision-making forums like citizens' juries or deliberative polls, which bring together random samples of citizens and trust them to make sense of issues and come to conclusions about them. Perhaps such forums reflect real-world potential for

---

4. C. Laborde, 'The Reception of John Rawls in Europe', *European Journal of Political Theory* 1 (2).
5. J. Rawls, 'The Idea of Public Reason Revisited', *The University of Chicago Law Review*, 64 (3), 1997.

the original position? Could this hypothetical device provide a goal that might reinvigorate representative institutions that are widely seen as distant and lacking deep credibility? Rawls wrote: 'Of course, when we try to simulate the original position in everyday life ... we will presumably find that our deliberations and judgements are influenced by our special inclinations and attitudes' (TJ, p147). Quite so. But even necessarily distant approximations might be vast improvements on current institutions.

Second, as the swing of ideological fashion comes back round again and the benefits of positive public ownership of key services are articulated in the UK and elsewhere, the radical character and moral force of Rawls's egalitarianism may serve as an ideological guide and inspiration. It seems to me that only those who would reject *wholesale* the market mechanism can regard Rawls's difference principle as a feeble device that would do little to rectify significant social inequalities. There will always be room for disagreement, but surely a Rawlsian state would be much less apologetic about not getting involved in the public/private partnership funding routine, would seek to control behaviour less and meet basic needs more, would fund health and education to levels comparable to the highest to be found elsewhere in Europe, and would at the same time be quite libertarian when it comes to lifestyles and the recognition of cultural difference.

And finally, underneath the decision-making procedures and the policy prescriptions, there is the Rawlsian vision of society as a sphere of social cooperation, part of a world where we 'value common institutions and activities as good in themselves' (TJ, p522). An anodyne statement on one level, perhaps, but in privatising times it may stand as a symbol of profound and almost radical social vision. Especially when we remind ourselves that, as Rawls wrote, 'The social system is not an unchangeable order beyond human control but a pattern of human action' (TJ, p102).

Christopher Hill

An appreciation

Norah Carlin

Christopher Hill, who died in February at the age of 91, was outstanding among British historians not only for his longevity, but for his intellectual productivity and for his resilience in the face of the many intemperate attacks he suffered throughout his career. Not many academics have published new books at the age of eighty-one and gone on to produce revised editions of their earlier work for some years thereafter, with carefully updated references and bibliographies and in the case of *The Intellectual Origins of the English Revolution*, with thirteen new chapters. Nor have many endured the kind of 'devastating assault upon his historical method, his historiographical achievement, and his intellectual integrity that would have stilled most other scholars' as Mark Kishlansky, one of the fiercest of his critics, once admitted.[1] The revival since Hill's death of stale accusations of 'spying' during his wartime employment at the Foreign Office, in a cheap attempt to gain publicity by an author who originally made these allegations in 1987, shows the depths to which some of his opponents could sink.[2]

In life, Hill faced his critics with equanimity, and went on producing intelligent and readable histories which have remained impressively popular with a mass audience looking for something more challenging than TV history. *Century of Revolution* has never been out of print since 1961, and *The World Turned Upside Down* has inspired wider enthusiasms for seventeenth-century radical culture - including the 1975 film *Winstanley*, songs by Leon Rosselson and Roy Bailey, and

---

1. Mark Kishlansky, 'Desert Island Radicals', in *Times Higher Education Supplement*, 7.9.84.
2. A. Glees, *The Secrets of the Service: British Intelligence and Communist Subversion, 1939-1951*; cf. *England's Turning Point*, p208.

more recently some of the music of the Levellers and Barnstormer bands.

What is so enduringly attractive about Hill's histories? Partly, his rare skill in making historical analysis as readable as narrative history; partly his palpable enthusiasm for the ferment of radical ideas in the mid-seventeenth-century revolution, and his willingness to examine apparently repellent or irrational ideas which contributed to the revolution as much as those which more directly appeal to modern readers. Hill's studies of religion in context went far beyond his sometimes clumsy attempts to relate Puritan ideas to the economic outlook of the 'middling sort'. His wider focus embraced the ways in which the people of the past used religious language to discuss their political, social, economic and aesthetic worlds: in short, the meanings which the people of the time gave to religion. 'The historian ignores at his peril a body of ideas which at one time aroused intense passion and controversy,' he wrote in *Antichrist in Seventeenth-Century England*. 'He must try to explain what lies behind ideological concepts which have lost their significance for him'. Thus he tackled not only the puritans' vehement anti-Catholicism, but also the violent Biblical language they regularly used. It is, as Hill points out, difficult to know how literally it was intended when even the Quakers, before 1661, used this kind of language. He argued for the connections between science and magic in the seventeenth century, pointing out that 'Newton did not share our hindsight knowledge that alchemy had no more secrets to reveal'. In this, he was discarding the earlier Marxist schema of a transhistorical battle between religion and science, which had been central to popular Marxist views of history for much of the twentieth century.[3]

If at times Hill seemed to reduce religion to a hollow shell whose meaning depended entirely on how it was used, his work nevertheless offers some effective arguments against the current fashion for religious essentialism which has followed John Morrill's attempt to rename the revolution 'England's wars of religion'. Even historians of seventeenth-century radicalism, including David Wootton and Andrew Sharp, now take 'religion' as a self-explanatory essence trumping all other categories, ignoring the difficulty that religion has meant different things in different societies, and that much of what we would

---

3. *People and Ideas in 17th Century England* (Brighton, 1986), p 274; Bill Schwarz, '"The people" in history: the Communist Party Historians' Group, 1946-56' in Richard Johnson et al (eds), *Making Histories: Studies in History-writing and Politics* (London, 1982), pp56-7.

now call politics was in the seventeenth century seen as religion. Hill pointed out, in *The English Bible and the Seventeenth-Century Revolution*, that the identification of religion and politics and the unity of church and state in early modern England might mean, paradoxically, that it was not a more religious but a less religious age than our own. Exploring the connections between religion, politics, economics, aesthetics and science, a project he described as 'total history', became central to his perception of Marxism.

Hill was one of the best known Marxist historians in Britain, but his was a remarkably fluid Marxism. In a rare reflection on his own historical practice, prompted by the rash of 'premature obsequies' for Marxism in 1991, he said that when asked whether he was a Marxist he would reply, 'What do you mean by Marxism?' He preferred 'to describe myself as Marxist influenced', and admitted that some of his earlier work had used 'Marxist jargon', which he would now think 'wholly inappropriate', but he denied that he had ever believed in 'a body of dogma to which I want to make history conform'.[4] Hill's development since leaving the Communist Party in 1957 had involved more than discarding the jargon, however. It is impossible to find a single, stable overall interpretation of the English revolution in his work. In the first version of his classic essay on the English revolution, published in 1940, it appears as a revolution made by the growing 'big bourgeoisie' in alliance with 'progressive landowners'; in the 1955 revised edition of this essay 'capitalist farmers' play more of a part; but in *The Good Old Cause* in 1969 the gentry triumph as the 'natural rulers' of the countryside. In *The Century of Revolution* (1961), the conflict appears as a three-way one: 'there was a quarrel between two groups of the ruling class; but looking on was the many-headed monster [the common people] which might yet be *tertius gaudens*'. Much of his later work was devoted to this 'third force' struggling for the 'revolution that didn't happen' rather than the one that did. Since 1980 he has argued that for Marxists a bourgeois revolution 'does *not* mean a revolution made or consciously willed by the bourgeoisie', but one whose outcome was conditions favourable to the continuing development of capitalism.[5]

---

4. *England's Turning Point*, pp291-2.
5. J.G.A. Pocock (ed.), *Three British Revolutions* (Princeton, NJ, 1980), pp130-2; *England's Turning Point*, p293.

'Clio has many mansions. Truth, Milton said, may have more shapes than one', Hill remarked appropriately in the same article. In an interesting article two years earlier, on 'scepticism, values and the historian', he had written that there is 'no right kind of history, any more than there is a historical truth which has been or is likely to be established.' 'The historian must ... be sceptical of the eternal validity of his or her own values,' he went on; and 'historians ... should be watched with the care with which we watch a suspected pickpocket'.[6] He never articulated any coherent theory which could tie such sceptical remarks to his own historical practice, however, and did not intervene in the 1980s 'poverty of theory' debate, initiated by EP Thompson. His position, though not explicitly theorised, is probably best described as the 'moderate realism' which satisfies many historians of the left today. He came to regard Marxism as a method, aiming to integrate cultural with political, social and economic history in a 'total history', rather than a fixed body of theory. Perhaps this comes closest to Raphael Samuel's suggestion that for some Marxists 'causality may be more fruitfully discussed by exploring relationships at a particular point in time between, say, business and politics ... rather than by pursuing a temporal sequence of developments'.[7] This kind of exploration was what Hill did best.

Another important element in Hill's conception of Marxism was 'history from below', now widely claimed as the most significant legacy of the Communist Party Historians' Group, in which he was a leading figure from its foundation in 1946 until 1957. Though his 1940 essay on the English revolution has seemed to many critics a prime example of mechanical Marxism, making history conform to the Marxist dogma of bourgeois revolution, it actually led to much argument within the Communist Party. It was even denounced in the party publication *Labour Monthly* - for deviating from the previous doctrine that English society became bourgeois under Tudor absolutism in the sixteenth century, and that the Civil War of 1642-8 was a response to Charles I's attempted 'counter-revolution'.[8] Hill's interpretation triumphed, however, and the growing influence of professional historians in the Communist Party led to the birth of

---

6. *England's Turning Point*, pp200, 206, 214.
7. Raphael Samuel, 'British Marxist historians, 1880-1980, Part One', *New Left Review*, 120 (1980), p95.
8. Alastair MacLachlan, *The Rise and Fall of Revolutionary England* (Basingstoke, 1996). An antagonistic but detailed account.

the Historians' Group.

Some see the work of Hill and others in the Historians' Group in this period as simply reflecting the prevailing Stalinism, fitting history into the procrustean bed of an evolutionary historical materialism dominated by a deterministic account of 'objective forces' bringing about progress and ultimately socialism. But the controversy over the 1940 essay demonstrates, in Bill Schwarz's view, that Hill and his allies stood for a more realistic history, and for one that prioritised human agency and class struggle. Hill did do much ephemeral historical writing for party publications in these years, comparing the pro-American foreign policy of post-war Britain to the pro-Spanish policies of the early Stuarts, Lysenko to Francis Bacon and so on, and including the obligatory references to Stalin. But these were also the years in which he wrote some of his most celebrated and enduring essays, such as 'The Norman Yoke', republished in 1958 in *Puritanism and Revolution*.

A more positive assessment of the Communist Party Historians' Group emphasises their swing away from the impersonal paradigm of the natural scientists to a view of history as a creative process, a struggle for freedom and self-emancipation by the masses. Integrating cultural history with historical materialism and appropriating the traditions of popular radicalism in England as a 'people's history' were central aims of the group, and these have had an enduring impact, long outlasting the 1950s *British Road to Socialism* politics with which they were initially linked. Bill Schwarz has suggested that the group's members largely failed to appreciate 'the extent to which the popular was a *construction* within the historiography, and not a self-evident reality which could be scooped up from the past'.[9] But Hill's 'Norman Yoke' essay (in its 1958 form) does show how the class basis of this 'popular' tradition changed with the development of capitalist society and the industrial working class, finally breaking the continuity which had linked seventeenth-century Levellers and nineteenth-century radicals.

Hill's work has influenced many other scholars over the years as well as reaching a wider public. Studies which interrelate the politics, religion and economics of the 'middling sort' in and around the seventeenth-century English

---

9. Schwarz, 'The people in history' (see note 3) - where 'The Norman Yoke', in its original 1954 version, is read differently.

Revolution continue to flourish (See, for example, Tim Harris (Ed.), *The Politics of the Excluded* (Basingstoke 2001). One of his nastier critics, J.C.D. Clark, claimed in his 1986 *Revolution and Rebellion* that the debate on the English Revolution 'is one between generations; it will be resolved in the way all such debates have to be settled'. Sadly, Christopher Hill is dead now, but the debate lives on, and will do so long after the Thatcher generation of historians have in their turn become 'Old Hat'.

A brief bibliography

Hill's writings are far too many, and too much complicated by revisions and re-editions, to attempt a full bibliography in a small space. The following list includes what seem to me to be his key works and the most useful collections of his essays. All titles by Christopher Hill unless otherwise indicated.

The English Revolution 1640: Three Essays (ed. Christopher Hill, London, 1940). Hill's own essay in this volume was substantially revised and published on its own as *The English Revolution 1640* (London, 1955).
The Century of Revolution, 1603-1714 (London, 1958): a popular textbook which has gone through many reissues but no radical revision.
The World Turned Upside Down (London, 1972) and *Antichrist in Seventeenth-Century England* (Oxford, 1990) and *The English Bible and the Seventeenth-Century Revolution* (London, 1993) are the major examples of Hill's approach to cultural history.
The Collected Essays of Christopher Hill (Brighton, 1984-6) consists of three volumes of essays originally written from 1958 onwards: I: *Writing and Revolution in Seventeenth-Century England* (1984). II: *Religion and Politics in Seventeenth-Century England* (1985), III: *People and Ideas in Seventeenth-Century England* (1986).
England's Turning Point (London, 1998): a useful collection of essays, some not previously published, dating from 1938 to 1994.

In addition, the following are useful:

Among negative academic criticisms of Hill, John Morrill, 'Christopher Hill's revolution', in his *The Nature of the English Revolution* (London, 1993 - generous as well as critical.
Alistair Maclachlan, *The Rise and Fall of Revolutionary England* (Basingstoke, 1996), crudely and obsessively anti-marxist, but valuable for the very full account he gives of Hill's pre-1957 writings.
Joyce Appleby, Lynn Hunt and Margaret Jacob, *Telling the Truth about History* (New York, 1994), for the 'moderate realist' position which theorises the kind of practice exemplified by Hill.

The making of political identity

Edward Thompson and William Cobbett

Michael Rustin

Mike Rustin looks at the crucial role played William Cobbett in the formation of Edward Thompson's identity as a writer and a radical.

In 1831 William Cobbett wrote an open letter to the Yeoman Militia who had been called out to suppress the Captain Swing disturbances in the countryside. Cobbett argued that these crimes could not be blamed on the 'the vicious disposition of the working people.' 'No, this cannot be the cause,' he wrote. 'The people are of the same make and nature that they always were ... There must therefore be some *other cause* or causes to produce these dreadful acts in a people the most just, the most good natured, the most patient in the world'. 'The great and general cause', Cobbett continued, 'is the *extreme poverty* of the working people; or, in other words, the *starving state* in which they are. That Bible, which they had been taught to read, as the means of saving their *souls*, tells them, from one end to the other, that their *bodies* are also not to be left to perish for want, while the land abounds with plenty, and that plenty arising too, from *their own labour*' (*Twopenny Trash*, 1 November 1831, pp97-8). Cobbett showed courage here, in coming to the defence of those driven to arson and other violent acts of protest in the rural Captain Swing rebellions, at a time when most of the press were righteously indignant about the protests.

Soundings

Here is Cobbett two months later, once more addressing himself to the great fear about these same disturbances, but this time to more prosperous people:

To the Yeoman Cavalry: On the Fires

I cannot call you friends, and I will not call you gentlemen. This plague of the country is now raging with greater fury than ever, and I think it proper to address you on the subject. You are called *yeoman cavalry; though perhaps more than half of you are loan-mongers, tax-gatherers, dead-weight people, stock-jobbers, shag-bag attorneys, bailiffs (mostly Scotch), toad-eating shopkeepers, who are ready to perform military duty towards the 'lower orders' in order at once to give evidence of your gentility, and to show your gratitude towards your rich customers for their paying your long bills without scruple. A very great part of you come in under one or the other part of this description; but to those of you who are farmers; that is to say who have land in your occupation; and who grow corn, and rear cattle, and who have barns, ricks and other things, liable to be set fire to; to you only do I address myself upon this occasion, being well aware that my arguments would produce no impression whatever upon your comrades above-mentioned* (Twopenny Trash, 1 January 1832, pp145-46).

In 'Sir, Writing by Candlelight' (*New Society*, 24 December 1970, republished in *Writing by Candlelight*, hereinafter referred to as *Candlelight*), Edward Thompson too addressed himself to the middle classes in their role of guardians of law and order, though he is concerned with the construction of moral panic through the correspondence columns of *The Times* rather than with the volunteer militia.

Nine years later, in 1979, this was his response to the majority reaction to the disturbances of the 'Winter of Discontent', which ushered in the Thatcher Governments:

Let the power workers dim the street lamps, or even plunge whole districts into utter darkness, the lights of righteousness and duty burn all the brighter from 10,000 darkened drawing-rooms in Chelsea or the Surrey Hills.
'*Sir,*
May I, writing by candlelight, express my total support for the government in their attempt to halt the unbelievably inflated wage claims now being made?'

The making of political identity

inquired one correspondent to *The Times* (12 December). Undoubtedly he may and will (*Candlelight*, p39).

Thompson is describing 'an epistolary *levée en masse*' of the readers of *The Times*, though in passing he refers to the 'true, physical levées en masse of the bourgeoisie against the plebs (The Volunteers against the Jacobins in 1800, the Yeomanry against the poor of Peterloo, the Specials against the Chartist 10 April, the debs and Oxbridge undergraduates against the General Strike).'

The Yeomanry referred to by Thompson are the self-same forces against whom Cobbett was writing twelve years after Peterloo. Thompson, like Cobbett, contrasts the lives of ordinary citizens to the fevered representations in the minds of the middle classes.

Thompson's version of everyday life and its needs is, however, a fully modern one:

> The grand lesson of the 'emergency' was this; the intricate reciprocity of human needs and services - a reciprocity of which we are, every day, the beneficiaries. In our reified mental world we think we are dependent upon *things*. What other people do for us is mediated by inanimate objects; the switch, the water tap, the lavatory chain, the telephone receiver, the cheque through the post. That cheque is where the duties of the good bourgeois end. But let the switch, or the tap, the chain or the receiver fail, and then the bourgeois discovers - at once - enormous 'oughts' within the reciprocal flow. But these 'oughts' are always the moral obligations of other people; the sewage workers ought not to kill fish, the dustmen ought not to encourage rats, the power workers ought not to imperil invalids, and - this week it will be - the postmen ought not to deny bronchitic old-age pensioners their Christmas parcels from grandchildren in Australia. Why, all these people owe a duty to the 'community.'

What the duty of the community is to these people is less firmly stated (*Candlelight*, p47).

Thompson and Cobbett

There are far more index references (59) to William Cobbett than to anyone else in Thompson's *The Making of the English Working Class* (hereinafter referred to as *Making*), where Cobbett is also the subject of what is in effect a separate and generally admiring chapter (part II of chapter 16). He was a source whose method was in some ways very congenial to Edward Thompson. Cobbett's writing was always full of detail, was drawn from observation and experience, and was based on a deep and personal identification with the circumstances of the labouring people to whom he felt both an attachment and a moral responsibility.[1] The rural labourers and independent farmers of Cobbett's England were transmuted as subjects of political identification in Thompson's experience - and that of the British Communist tradition - into an urban working class, known and admired through their most articulate representatives through the Party and through adult education. *The Making of the English Working Class* of course describes the transformation of Cobbett's rural labourers into the urban working class of the nineteenth and early twentieth centuries. The essays in Thompson's *Customs in Common* describe the erosion of a morally-regulated agricultural economy, to the defence of whose traditional responsibilities and decencies (as he saw them) Cobbett's life was devoted. The game laws, which are one of the main subjects of *Whigs and Hunters*, had also been an important issue for Cobbett, who defended the right of the people to take wild animals, and who attacked the barbarous punishments meted out to those who defied the laws. And Thompson's insistence, in later controversies, on the virtues of empiricism had as its model not only the scientific empiricism of Darwin, or Marx, but also the writer's and journalist's empiricism of Cobbett, rooted in his experience, observations and feelings. Thompson writes of one passage of Cobbett: 'Everything here is solid, and related, not to a literary culture, but to commonly available experience' (*Making*, p823). And of another passage:

> ... wherever he was, Cobbett always compelled his readers, by the immediacy of his vision, the confusion of reflection and description, the solidity of detail and the physical sense of place, to identify themselves with his own

---

1. Cobbett is plainly aware of substantial differences of status and condition between himself and the labourers. Membership in a common moral community does not imply equality for Cobbett. This is one important point of continuity with his earlier days as a Tory.

standpoint. And 'standpoint' is the proper word, for Cobbett placed himself firmly in some physical setting - on his farm at Botley or on the road into Tenterden - and then led outwards from the evidence of his senses to his general conclusions (*Making* p827).

Cobbett is certainly a strong representative, in Thompson's mind, of the 'empirical idiom' which he later defends in his great polemics first with Perry Anderson and Tom Nairn, then with Louis Althusser, distinguishing this habit of thought from the ideology of empiricism. Thompson's identification with Cobbett, his imaginative presence in the formation of Thompson's own political voice, seems to have been very deep. He said, after all that:

> It was Cobbett who *created* this Radical intellectual culture, not because he offered the most original ideas, but in the sense that he found the tone, the style, and the arguments which could bring the weaver, the schoolmaster, and the shipwright, into a common discourse (*Making*, p820).

There is no doubt that this was one of Thompson's aspirations as a political writer throughout his life, and one which he sometimes brought off. He wrote that 'Cobbett was the free-born Englishman incarnate' (p824). There could hardly be higher praise from Thompson - though he is also objective and balanced in noting Cobbett's limitations as a political leader.

What he found in Cobbett's writings, and which it seems to me had a great influence on his own identity as a writer and political figure, was a way of experiencing himself as a public person, that is to say a way of relating to events, to opponents, and to a democratic public. What he was able to learn from Cobbett was above all in the dimensions of identity.

What are the features of this identity? Well, in the first place, as Thompson points out, it had a personal voice - and the writing of both Cobbett and Thompson is often most effective when this 'voice' is most clearly established. Cobbett intended much of his writing to be read aloud, no doubt often to those who were unable to read him for themselves. One can often hear the forms of speech through his prose - George Spater, one of his recent biographers, has pointed out that 'most of Cobbett's writing is the spoken word which has happened to find its way into print.'² Another biographer, Ian Dyck, has pointed out that *Rural Rides* is among other things the report of the journey of a political organiser, giving speeches mainly to farmers in the towns that he visits, and put up for the night by different 'friends', personally known and unknown.³ Cobbett, though he is fairly discreet about it in *Rural Rides*, was not on the road solely to collect material for his writing. This is reminiscent of more modern political speaking tours, of which Thompson himself had several kinds of experience, in his Communist, New Left, and peace campaigning days.

Cobbett, writing his hundreds of thousands of words of journalism, turned the construction of this 'voice' into a considerable art. Much of his writing, in the *Political Register*, took the form of the 'address' - that is a communication from himself to some identified person or designated group of persons. Cobbett wrote these addresses in his own person, and is often highly self-referential. He can presume, as the writer and editor of a weekly publication, *Cobbett's Political Register*, that his readers remember some of what he had written before, and that these public debates have their history. *Rural Rides* uses the format of a diary or travel memoir, and through the writerly device of his reported journey is able to hold together a variety of reflections and kinds of subject-matter without awkwardness - for example, political polemic, topographical reflection, and his continuing survey of the condition of the land. He uses his eyes as he goes along, he encounters individuals whom can interrogate, his thoughts are provoked by names and reputations - for example of the owners of the land he crosses or passes by. But above all he has his ceaseless flow of observations - didactic, indignant, quizzical, reflective or appreciative of the beauty or comeliness of what he sees. It is in these personal ways, by establishing his presence as a witness or interlocutor, that Cobbett establishes his authority to speak for those without public voices.

> In quitting FRANT I descended into a country *more wooded* than that behind me. I asked a man whose fine woods those were that I pointed to, and I fairly gave a *start*, when he said, 'the MARQUIS CAMDEN'S.' Milton talks of the

---

2. 'A large part was dictated - dictated and not read - for he rarely looked over what he had written either when he put it down himself or when it was taken down by others.' George Spater, *William Cobbett: the Poor Man's Friend*, Vol. 1, Cambridge University Press 1982, p2.
3. Ian Dyck, *William Cobbett and Rural Popular Culture*, Cambridge University Press 1992.

Leviathan in a way to make one draw in one's shoulders with fear; and I appeal to anyone, who has been at sea when a whale has come near the ship, whether he has not, at the first sight of this monster, made a sort of involuntary movement, as if to *get out of the way*. Such was the movement that I now made. However, soon coming to myself, on I walked my horse by the side of my pedestrian informant. It is BAYHAM ABBEY that this great and awful sinecure placeman owns in this part of the country. Another great estate he owns near *Sevenoaks*. But here alone he spreads his length and breadth over more, they say, than *ten or eleven thousand acres of land*, great part of which consists of oak-woods. But, indeed, what estates might he not purchase? Not much less than *thirty years* he held a place, a sinecure place, that yielded him about THIRTY THOUSAND POUNDS A-YEAR! At any rate he, according to Parliamentary accounts, has received, of public money, LITTLE SHORT OF A MILLION OF GUINEAS. These, at 30 guineas an acre, would buy *thirty thousand acres of land*. And, what did he have all this money *for*? Answer me that question, WILBERFORCE, you who called him a 'bright star', when he gave up *a part* of his enormous sinecure. He gave up all but the *trifling* sum of nearly *three thousand pounds a-year*! What a *bright star*! And *when* did he give it up? When the *radicals* had made the country ring with it. When his name was, by their means, getting into every mouth in the kingdom; when every radical speech and petition contained the name of CAMDEN. Then it was, and not till then, that this *'bright star,'* let fall part of its *'brilliancy.'* So that Wilberforce ought to have thanked the *radicals*, and not CAMDEN (*Rural Rides*, pp176-7).

Cobbett was able through his writing to hold together different aspects of his relationship to his public. He can move in a single passage from the role of tribune and defender of the people against Old Corruption, to that of a kind of WEA teacher of matters agricultural. For example, in the issue of his *Twopenny Trash* for April 1831, Cobbett writes an address to 'The Labourers of England.' He begins by reminding his readers about the fate of two labourers, Joseph and Robert Mason of Bullington (one of the 'little hard parishes' in the north of Hampshire), who had been 'transported for life, having been condemned to death'. These, wrote Cobbett, were 'perfectly sober and honest men', men of whom it 'was proved they read Cobbett's Register and Cobbett's History of the

Protestant Reformation', and who had been found guilty of riot against the conditions of the 'hard parishes'. (Cobbett felt a particular responsibility for the fate of these two men, since he thought that they had been sentenced severely and unjustly because of this suspected association with his campaigns.) He goes on to welcome the impending Parliamentary Reform, whilst pleading with his readers not to expect too much of it too soon. But he concludes his address with an intense and rather inspiring piece of instruction concerning the cultivation of a dwarf form of Indian Corn, which he says was brought into England by his eldest son:

> Now, my friends, this *bacon* being the standard with me, I am about to give you instructions how to get more bacon that you would not be able to get without those instructions. I am not conceited enough to think that I can tell you anything useful concerning those things which you have been accustomed to from your infancy; but I am going to tell you about something that you cannot know anything about. I am going to tell you how to get the means of fatting a pig of ten score, without peas, beans, barley or oats ...
>
> **Instructions to Labourers for Raising Cobbett's Corn**
> I will first describe this corn to you. It is that which is sometimes called corn; and sometimes people call it Indian wheat. It is that sort of corn which the disciples ate as they were going up to Jerusalem on the Sabbath day. They gathered it in the fields as they went along, and ate it green, they being 'an hungered', for which, you know, they were reproved by the Pharisees. I have written a treatise on this corn, in a book which I sell for two and sixpence, giving a minute account of the qualities, the culture, the harvesting, and the various uses of this corn; but I shall here confine myself to what is necessary for a labourer to know about it, so that he may be induced to raise, and may be enabled to raise enough of it in his garden to fat a pig of ten score (*Twopenny Trash*, 1831, p229).

Modern adult education lecturers - and of course Thompson was once one such - might wish sometimes that what they had to teach was as immediately useful to their pupils as this. Cobbett addresses his readers at the end of this lesson,

The making of political identity

acknowledging the strangely public and impersonal nature of what in other respects feels to him like a relationship between persons:

> You must be quite sensible that I cannot have any motive but your good in giving you this advice, other than the delight that I take and the pleasure which I derive from doing that good. You are all personally unknown to me: in all human probability not one man in a thousand will ever see me. You have no more power to show your gratitude to me than you have to cause me to live for a hundred years. I do not desire that you should deem this a favour received from me. The thing is worth your trying at any rate (p233).

After this reflection on the impersonal nature of mass communication, Cobbett concludes in practical mode, listing fifty gentlemen to whom he has promised to send parcels of corn seed, to pass on to such labourers as they may choose, together with his little manual of instruction. Among those named is the widow Mason, the mother of the two transported labourers he has mentioned earlier. Cobbett makes frequent reference in his writings to the individual victims of government and judicial oppression, those who have been unjustly hanged or transported, to ensure that they are not forgotten. His two year term of imprisonment in Newgate was for his 'seditious' protests against the flogging of allegedly mutinous soldiers. His solidarity with the victims of the oppressive judicial system was an important basis for the people's trust in him. His practice of telling in print the stories of these individual sufferers from injustice pioneered the activity of later radical journalists in exposing individual abuses of the law.

Cobbett's practice of identifying or naming individuals who are to stand as representatives of his larger audience (an important aspect of his writing in *Rural Rides*) puts one in mind of the numerous techniques used by the mass media today to represent public events in meaningful individual terms. These methods include television reportage, vox pop interviews, 'question times' with studio audiences, and documentary drama (of course the degree to which they provide a genuine voice for people is variable). However, the problem of making public events meaningful to audiences in personal terms is inseparable from mass democracy and mass communication. Cobbett was a pioneer of many forms of popular writing - the open letter to a public figure (the opening step in an imaginary dialogue), the political column (with its identifiable voice or style), the manual of popular instruction, the travel memoir, the popular history.

As we have seen, he could combine these genres. His *English Grammar*, for example, used its examples to provide some political amusement well as instruction in language, as in the following, quoted by George Spater, where Cobbett refers to nouns of number: 'Such as Mob, Parliament, Rabble, House of Commons, Regiment, Court of King's Bench, Den of Thieves, and the like.' And, in relation to the Queen Caroline quarrel, Cobbett writes: 'The Queen *defies* the tyrants; the Queen *defied* the tyrants; the Queen *will defy* the tyrants'.

His *History of the Protestant Reformation* was among other things a defence of medieval Catholic ideas of moral responsibility for the poor, and an account of the origins of contemporary Whig jobbery in the expropriation of the monasteries. What held this prodigious variety of writings together was Cobbett's strong sense of self and voice. As Thompson pointed out in *The Making*, this style of personalisation which worked so well for Cobbett provided rather an unfortunate model for his radical successors, encouraging divisiveness and egotism when solidarity and cooperation were needed. Whereas it was perhaps only possible for a radical public to be initially gathered together by a powerful and self-confident personality such as Cobbett, its next stage of development required more collective approaches, which, as Thompson pointed out, were somewhat alien to Cobbett himself.[4]

Cobbett's 'addresses' in the *Political Register* and the *Twopenny Trash* were to two distinct kinds of subject. One was the people or an identified body of them - for example, 'To the Journeymen and Labourers of England, Scotland, and Ireland', 'To the Good and True Men of Hampshire, on the riotous proceedings at the Winchester Meeting', 'To the Industrious Classes, on the Causes of the Present Poverty and Misery', 'To the Thinking People of England', etc. These designations are of proto-classes (at the moment of their 'making'), somewhere

---

4. Thompson's own role in the British new left in the late 1950s and early 1960s has been criticised for similar failings of over-personalisation. At a public level, these polemics could achieve a high level of eloquence and biting wit, and elicit responses of exemplary lucidity, as can be seen from Thompson's arguments with Perry Anderson and Tom Nairn, the second generation of editors of *New Left Review,* reprinted in *The Poverty of Theory,* and from Anderson's reply in his *Arguments within English Marxism* (1980). See Michael Kenny, *The First New Left,* Lawrence and Wishart 1995, for a thoughtful and well-researched account of this history.

between a populist identification of the people as a whole, as against their rulers, and of one social class as against another.

The other form of address was open letters to his major adversaries, 'To Parson Malthus, on the Population of England,' 'To William Wilberforce, on the State of the Cotton Factory Labourers, and on the Speech of Andrew Ryding, who cut Horrocks with a cleaver', 'To the Duke of Wellington, on the great good which will arise from his Measure relative to small notes', and even 'To the President of the United States'. (One recalls Bertrand Russell's Open Letters to Heads of State about the dangers of nuclear war as a later example of this genre.)

In these addresses to public men, Cobbett responds to their Parliamentary speeches, or to their influential writings, constituting himself as a tribune of the people, answering what he regards as false and mischievous political positions. He often reports his opponents' positions and speeches at length, making a point of his willingness to let readers see both sides of an argument, whilst the authorities resort on their side to gagging and censorship. Cobbett, as Raymond Williams pointed out, was a pioneer of the reporting of Parliamentary Debates.[5] But this willingness to report his opponents' views does not make Cobbett polite about them:

TO PARSON MALTHUS
On the Rights of the poor and on the cruelty recommended by him to be exercised toward the poor. *Political Register*, May 1819

PARSON,
I have, during my life, detested many men; but never anyone so much as you. Your book on POPULATION contains matter more offensive to my feelings even than that of the Dungeon-Bill. It could have sprung from no mind not capable of dictating greater cruelty than any recorded in the history of the massacre of St Bartholomew. Priests have, in all age, been remarkable for cool and deliberate and unrelenting cruelty; but it seems to have been reserved for the Church of England to produce one who has a just claim to the atrocious

---

5. Raymond Williams, *Cobbett*, Oxford University Press 1983.

pre-eminence. No assemblage of words can give an appropriate designation of you; and, therefore, as being the single word which best suits the character of such a man, I call you *Parson*, which, amongst other meanings, includes that of Boroughmonger tool ...

In your book you show that, in certain cases, a *crowded* population has been attended with great evils, a great deal of unhappiness, misery, and human degradation. You then, without any reason to bear you out, predict, or leave it to be clearly inferred, that the same is likely to take place in England. Your principles are almost all false; and your reason, in almost any instance, is the same. But it is not my intention to waste time upon your abstract matter. I shall come, at once, to your practical result, to your recommendation to the Boroughmongers to pass laws to *punish the poor for marrying*.

After quoting from Malthus's argument and refuting it on several counts, Cobbett goes on to dismiss his idea that there had even *been* a large increase of population (it was this belief that justified Malthus's attacks on poor relief and on all attempts to raise the living standards of the poor). Cobbett noted changes in statistical classifications, the apparent absurdity of the rate of growth reported, but he then, typically, asks his readers to look to the evidence of their own eyes to prove to themselves that Malthus must have been wrong. He points out that the size of the rural churches that everyone sees all around the country clearly shows that there must have been large congregations to fill them in the past:

> Then, if we take a look back, we shall find that in 1600 there could have been only about a couple of million of people in the country; that a couple of hundred years before there could have been no people at all in the country, or, only two or three pairs turned down as breeders, at any rate; and then, how the devil came the churches? They were built four hundred years before that; and will you, PARSON, undertake to make us believe that the churches were built without there being any body to go to them; that they were built, too, without hands ...

Cobbett characteristically adds that even though there are supposed never to have been large congregations, nevertheless tithes are levied to support large benefices and livings for the clergy - like 'Parson Malthus'. The passage reads, and was probably written, as a speech in an imaginary debate with Malthus. The assumption of such arguments as these is that opponents do have something to say, which needs to be made known in its own terms, and then refuted. Incidentally, Thompson describes these kinds of writing as Cobbett's polemics, 'polemic' becoming one of Thompson's favourite terms. Another presupposition of this writing is that political debate essentially takes place between prominent individuals, who stand personally for social interests of various kinds. Cobbett had won the right to define himself in these terms as the representative of the popular interest, of the 'free born Englishman'. This is a political world in which influence is exercised by, and debate takes place between *notables*. Cobbett is writing at, and of course creating, that transitional moment at which it became possible to become such a notable by establishing oneself as a popular journalist or orator.

Thompson was drawn strongly himself to this role of the individual advocate and polemicist, attempting to embody in his political writings and speeches the voice of larger unheard publics. There sometimes seemed to be something anachronistic about this personalisation of political debate, which did not fit well with the modern world of organised party politics. Political parties spoke in slogans, in 'party lines', later in 'soundbites' attended by 'spin-doctors', not by reasoned argument and in individual polemics. Thompson denounced the hypocrisies of both orthodox Communist and Social Democratic parties, and the decadence of their debates. The first new left, and the nuclear disarmament campaign in its two phases, tried to construct an alternative public space in which such political arguments could be heard. But it was difficult for individuals, however eloquent and charismatic, or for loosely organised 'movements', to make a sustained impact on this political culture, or even to find an acknowledged space within it. How could someone like Edward Thompson conduct a public political argument with a Michael Stewart, or Fred Mulley, or John Nott - when *all* the party apparatuses wanted to prevent such arguments taking place on public platforms, since it would endanger their own monopoly of political space, and when many of the party functionaries in these roles could in any case hardly begin to sustain such a level of debate. Thompson himself complained of this situation:

> These questions can't be asked in that set of frames. They aren't proper 'political' questions. This is partly because of the insufferable arrogance of the major political parties. Long ago they had the audacity, through parliamentary

control of broadcasting, to confiscate this part of the nation's intellectual life to themselves. Politics was defined as party politics, and then it was carved up, unequally, between them.

If John Milton or William Hazlitt were still around, and wanted to break in a with a question of why or where, the managers of all the parties would gang up to keep them off. On every side a producer has to skirt around all these fenced-in estates with their party-political gamekeepers and notices saying 'PRIVATE - TRESPASSERS KEEP OUT' (*The Heavy Dancers*, p3).

One of the attractions for Thompson of work with the dissenting movements of Eastern Europe, both in his earlier days as a dissident Communist, and later in the European peace movement, was - paradoxically - that in that authoritarian political context individual intellectuals and artists were able to have a more significant role as spokespersons for the people than they were in the democratic west, where political communication is routinised and instrumentalised, as a form of public relations. (New Labour seems to be even more single-minded about this than Old Labour was.) Dissenting politics in Eastern Europe transcended this pattern for a few years, but these nations now seem to have expelled their artists and intellectuals from political life, and to have defaulted to the professionalised party discourses of the Western type.

The first 'new left' attempted to create a political space of the kind Thompson advocated, and its failure was a damaging one so far as debate about democratic alternatives was concerned. A number of splits and divisions of political labour followed. Marxist militants found themselves confined mainly to sects, intellectuals were contained within the universities, and others who looked for more mainstream politics had to struggle in the anaerobic atmosphere of the Labour Party. Thompson was comfortable with none of these roles, remaining remote from both party and sect. And having been involved in a vigorous campaign in 1970 at Warwick University, against the new managerialism of the 'business university' (this concept really came into its own later on), he soon resigned from his academic post, preferring to work as an independent scholar.[6] This liking for the role of a writer, polemicist, historian, and intellectual, over an institutional role, is something else which

---

6. See *Warwick University Limited*, Penguin 1970.

links Thompson to Cobbett.

The second great phase of the nuclear disarmament movement, and Thompson's involvement as the leading figure of END, the European Campaign for Nuclear Disarmament, did make it possible for him to find a significant public role in the early 1980s. This phase brought a flow of political writings, two or three of which are classics. Several of these pieces were constructed as arguments with representative public figures or intellectuals of the establishment. Thompson made a major contribution to the understanding of the nuclear arms race, developing the new theory of 'exterminism'. This was the idea of a reciprocally reinforcing military-industrial system, whose technical developments edge the world ever closer to final catastrophe. The idea of a 'mode of exterminism' was an important step in Thompson's continuing evolution away from economistic Marxism, since it attributed to the military systems of the two sides the capacity to drive their entire social systems. It was because these debates had some serious intellectual substance that Thompson's arguments with leading theorists of deterrence, such as Sir Michael Howard, were conducted with overt respect on his side, if with devastating irony.

In *Protest and Survive*, the brilliant polemic occasioned by the government's civil defence pamphlet *Protect and Survive*, Thompson replies to a letter to *The Times* by Howard, which had advocated civil defence as necessary to the credibility of the nuclear deterrent:

We are now at last prepared to cast a more realistic eye upon Professor Howard's scenario.

According to this, the 'initially limited Soviet strike' might, in the absence of civil defence precautions, create conditions of 'political turbulence' which would prevent 'us' from using our own nuclear weapons in retaliation. This would be regrettable, since it would inhibit the escalation from 'tactical' to 'theatre' to 'second strike', sea-based nuclear war. But he envisages civil defence measures 'on a scale sufficient to give protection to a substantial number of the population', enabling this number to endure the 'disagreeable consequences' which would ensure.

The object of civil defence, then, is not so much to save lives as to reduce the potential for 'political turbulence' of those surviving the first strike, in order to enable 'us' to pass over to a second and more fearsome stage of nuclear warfare. It is Professor Howard's merit that he states this sequence honestly, as realistic, and even that he allows that the consequences will be disagreeable.

Thompson characterised the practical advice given by the government:

... The population of this country, however, will not be invited to these bunkers, and it is an Official Secret to say where they are. The population will be sent off, with a do-it-yourself booklet *(Protect and Survive)*, to wait in their own homes. They will be advised to go down to the ground floor or the cellar, and make a cubby-hole there with old doors and planks, cover it sandbags, books, and heavy furniture, and then creep into these holes with food and water for fourteen days, a portable ratio, a portable latrine, and, of course, a tin-opener.

Thompson notes, however, that the government has been cannier about the likely public response to preparations for major nuclear attacks than Howard himself:

I suspect that, for these reasons, Professor Howard is regarded, by public-relations-conscious persons in the Establishment, as a great patriot of NATO and an admirable fellow, but as an inexperienced politician. The people of the country have been made dull and stupid by a diet of Official Information. But they are not all *that* stupid, and there is still a risk - a small risk, but not one worth taking - that they might remember who they are, and become 'turbulent' before the war even got started. [7]

Thompson regarded the management of public opinion, by the use of Official Secrets legislation and the intimidation of dissidents, as a means of preparing populations not merely for nuclear deterrence, but for the possibility of

---

7. There is in Thompson's references here to the potentially turbulent people a hint of the way he inclined to self-dramatise the radical movements with which he identified. Even if dissent was not an overwhelming force, Thompson always needed to feel that it could become so. His sense of the real public he represented was nearly always more precarious and romanticised than Cobbett's relationship to his.

The making of political identity

nuclear war itself. He became concerned, as Cobbett had been during the French Wars, about the effects of military preparations and paranoia on civil liberties, and wrote vigorously about the secret state and its apparatus of spies and deceit, and about the individual victims of state intimidation and oppression.

In discussing apologists for the secret state, he was less polite than in his debate with the academic theorists of deterrence. His review of a book by Chapman Pincher, a journalist closely identified and linked with the intelligence agencies, was a polemical masterpiece. In it, Thompson produced a metaphorical flight equal to one of Cobbett's own.

> Mr Chapman Pincher has been employed for over thirty years as a sort of common conduit through which government ministers, senior civil servants and others have leaked their official secrets, scandals and innuendoes to their readers and to each other. He has now published an account of this commerce, called Inside Story. I have examined this work, less with an eye to the subject-matter (mainly Westminster and Whitehall trivia) than to Mr Pincher's style of operation.

The central figure of speech develops as the piece proceeds:

> ... we may suppose that Mr Pincher has been less an operator than a tool of other operators. In this view, we must suppose that no one has leaked Official Secrets improperly. All the leaking has been contrived and wholly proper. It has been an exercise of our superiors in the management of news; in which proper persons decide not only when an Official Secret becomes an Unsecret, but how it becomes an Unsecret for some, while it remains defended by criminal sanctions if published by others.
>
> This might be justified as an exercise in confusing and 'disinforming' the KGB, although in fact, as in the case of Burghfield, the real objective is to confuse, disinform and manage opinion in Britain.
>
> In this view, the columns of the Express may be seen as a kind of official urinal in which, side by side, high officials of MI5 and MI6, Sea Lords, Permanent Under-Secretaries, Lord George Brown, Chiefs of the Air Staff, nuclear scientists, Lord Wigg, and others, stand patiently leaking in the public

interest. One can only admire their resolute attention to these distasteful duties.

The occasion for this piece was the Official Secrets Trial against Crispin Aubrey, John Berry and Duncan Campbell. Its serious point was to demonstrate that Pincher had published classified materials, with detailed information, whose official sources he freely announced, and clearly with official sanction, which had they been published by anti-nuclear campaigners would have led to their trial and imprisonment.

One is reminded, in political substance, of Cobbett's defence of those harshly treated by the game laws, or in the repression of the Captain Swing disturbances, and of his vigorous denunciations of the tame press of the government. And in metaphorical form, of the wonderful passage, quoted in *The Making of the English Working Class*, in which Cobbett compares Brougham and the moderate reformers to scarecrows or Shoy-Hoys. He describes the homely functions of scarecrows in a field, and concludes:

> Just exactly such are the functions of our political shoy-hoys. The agricultural shoy-hoys deceive the depredating birds but a very short time; but they continue to deceive those who stick them up and rely upon them, who, instead of rousing in the morning, and sallying upon the depredators with powder and shot, trust to the miserable shoy-hoys and thus lose their corn and their seeds. Just thus it is with the people, who are the dupes of all political shoy-hoys. In Suffolk, and other eastern counties, they call them mawkses (quoted in *Making*, p825).

As Thompson argued and also demonstrated by example, it is possible to engage in and convey significant political thinking by means of metaphors whose power is their connection with readers' everyday experience.

Nevertheless, because of the difficulties of sustaining fundamental debate in the mainstream political arenas, the main objects of most of Thompson's great polemics were not his leading political contemporaries - grey figures for the most part by comparison with himself - but other political intellectuals of the left - Perry Anderson and Tom Nairn, Louis Althusser, Leslek Kolakowski - all figures relatively marginal to the British political scene. In these polemics,

Thompson achieved great heights of writing, combining wonderful and entertaining conceits and metaphors, with sustained theoretical arguments for a politics of self-activity guided by an understanding of the particularity of British history. He mocked, for example, Anderson and Nairn's negative view of British radical achievement:

And the essence of both authors' analysis of Labourism may be found in Anderson's phrase, 'In England, a supine bourgeoisie produced a subordinate proletariat'.
… There is about them, the air of an inverted Podsnappery.

'We Englishmen are Very Proud of our Constitution, Sir,' Mr Podsnap explained with a sense of meritorious proprietorship.
It was Bestowed Upon Us By Providence. No Other Country is as Favoured as This Country…'
'And other countries,' said the foreign gentleman. 'They do how?'
'They do, Sir,' returned Mr Podsnap, gravely shaking his head; 'they do - I am sorry to be obliged to say it - as they do.'

But now the roles are reversed. Mr Podsnap, who has swelled to engross all British culture over the past 400 years, is being arraigned in his turn.
'And other countries,' said Mr Podsnap remorsefully. 'They do how?'
'They do,' returned Messrs Anderson and Nairn severely: 'They do - we are sorry to be obliged to say it - in Every Respect Better. Their Bourgeois Revolutions have been Mature. Their Class Struggles have been Sanguinary and Unequivocal. Their Intelligentsia has been Autonomous and Integrated Vertically. Their Morphology has been Typologically Concrete. Their Proletariat has been Hegemonic.'
There is indeed throughout their analysis an undisclosed model of Other Countries, whose typological symmetry offers a reproach to British exceptionalism. Set against this model, the English working class is 'one of the enigmas of modern history,' the historical experience of the English bourgeoisie has been 'fragmented, incomplete,' English intellectuals have not constituted 'a true intelligentsia' ('The Peculiarities of the English', in *The Poverty of Theory*, pp36-7).

This was however the 'specialisation' or narrowcasting of the kind of argument that Thompson would have liked to see going on in every pub. But modern mass politics and communications do not allow much complexity in political debate. It is salutary to think that in the 1820s Cobbett's *Political Register* had, by the standards of the time, a mass circulation - a 50,000 weekly sale in a population of eight or nine million.

Repeated reference to the self in such writing is not always easy to bring off, and Edward Thompson, even in the fine piece about official secrets quoted above did not succeed all the way through. Cobbett's peculiar gift for writing about himself, but with a constant sense that what really mattered were the objects of his attention and feeling, and not himself, is very hard to emulate. It is perhaps his completely open acknowledgement of his pride in himself which is so disarming, at least in his public persona. (He is happy to tell his readers of how he was chaired in triumph from a public meeting, and can make an enjoyable anecdote of it.) There is no false modesty, no self-regard which is not open to view. Perhaps it was the intensity of Cobbett's relationship to so many projects and activities - his farm, his journalism, his public rows, his meetings, his hates, his books - which successfully contained his extraordinarily powerful sense of self. (The collapse of Cobbett's marriage and his quarrels with his children in his last years perhaps show the price that others paid for the long years of support demanded by this energetic but egotistical man.) Cobbett's incredible volume of activity and writing reminds one in this respect of Charles Dickens, in the next generation.

Sometimes Thompson was able to integrate in his writing this eloquently personal voice, with an engagement with an external subject sufficiently intense to justify a highly personal authorial presence. The pieces in which this is brought off seem to come out of the possibility of a real collective engagement, in which Thompson can legitimately feel that he speaks for more than himself, even when he speaks *as* himself. But these conditions are not easy to fulfil in contemporary political practice, and there are other writings where the touch - that is the implied relationship with his subject and his audience - is less sure.

Cobbett seemed to have a confidence in his knowledge of those he wrote about - a knowledge no doubt continually replenished by his travels - which it is hard for contemporary socialists and radicals to keep hold of. Thompson wrote eloquently enough of his comrades in the socialist movement and later in the peace movement, but sometimes his wishes for the movement he would have liked to see took precedence over accurate perceptions of what actually existed. This 'movement' was sometimes there in experience, and sometimes wasn't, and Thompson's political writing at times reflects these uncertainties.

Both for Cobbett and Thompson, writing seems to work best when the relationship to the subject is most intense and grounded - in agricultural life for Cobbett, and more often in his historical writing - rather than politics - for Thompson.

Thompson's historical and political writing plainly achieved the highest qualities of argument, evocation of experience, and theoretical subtlety. But it has another distinctive dimension too, which makes it quite unlike the work of most other historians and writers on politics. This can be understood in terms of the dimensions of the identity of the writer, and the identifications on which this is based. The past transmits itself to us in Thompson's writing not simply in what and who he writes about, but also in *how* he writes, and whose voices he remembers and recreates in doing so. Outstanding writers are perhaps most often formed by partial identification with their predecessors, and this certainly seems to have been the case for Thompson.

This has a collective dimension, since his achievement in *The Making of the English Working Class* was to re-discover and re-create for contemporary readers and political actors the 'voices' of the early English working class movement. It is through such writing that collective traditions are remembered and enabled to continue in a living form, as Thompson so memorably explained:

> I am seeking to rescue the poor stockinger, the Luddite cropper, the 'obsolete' hand-loom weaver, the 'utopian' artisan, and even the deluded follower of Joanna Southcott, from the enormous condescension of posterity (*Making*, p13).

But such identification also takes place at an individual level. It is through this process that the register and voice of a writer may be initially formed, and thus can become a root of his or her subsequent imaginative work. Cobbett was one

Soundings

such figure for Edward Thompson. (William Morris and William Blake, each the subject of major biographical works by Thompson, were two others, who shared with Cobbett the characteristic independence of mode of life and voice which Thompson achieved for himself.)

One hopes that the models of political writing based in experience which Cobbett established, and Thompson re-created in his own work, will be emulated by new generations of writers, for the sake of the democratic practice to which both Cobbett and Thompson gave a full commitment.

Works by Edward Thompson cited in this essay

The Making of the English Working Class, Penguin edition, 1968
Warwick University Limited, Penguin, 1970 (edited by Thompson)
Whigs and Hunters, Allen Lane, 1975
The Poverty of Theory, Merlin Press, 1978
Writing by Candlelight, Merlin Press, 1980
Protest and Survive, Penguin Special, 1980 (edited by Thompson and Dan Smith)
The Heavy Dancers, Merlin Press, 1985
Customs in Common, Penguin, 1991

Soundings

is now *freely* available *online* to all subscribers

Benefits include:

- Document to document linking using live references, for fast, reliable access to wider, related literature.
- Journal content that is fully searchable, across full text, abstracts, titles, TOCs and figures.
- Live links to and from major Abstract and Indexing resources to aid research.
- The ability to conduct full-text searching across multiple journals, giving you a wider view of the research that counts.
- Powerful TOC alerting services that keep you up to date with the latest research.

Set up access now at: www.ingentaselect.com/register.htm

and follow the online instructions*

Subscription Enquiries:
help@ingenta.com

*Access is provided by Ingenta Select, an Ingenta website

BACK ISSUES

Issue 1 – **Launch Issue** Stuart Hall, Beatrix Campbell, Fred Halliday, Mae-Wan Ho, Barbara Castle, Simon Edge.

Issue 2 – **Law & Justice** Kate Markus, Keir Starmer, Ken Wiwa, Kader Asmal, Mike Mansfield, Jonathan Cooper, Ethan Raup, John Griffith, Keith Ewing, Ruth Lister, Anna Coote, Steven Rose, Jeffrey Weeks.

Issue 3 – **Heroes & Heroines** Barbara Taylor, Jonathan Rutherford, Graham Dawson, Becky Hall, Anna Grimshaw, Simon Edge, Kirsten Notten, Susannah Radstone, Graham Martin, Cynthia Cockburn, Anthony Barnett.

Issue 4 – **The Public Good** Gail Lewis, Francie Lund, Pam Smith, Loretta Loach, John Clarke, Jane Falkingham, Paul Johnson, Will Hutton, Charlie King, Anne Simpson, Brigid Benson, Candy Stokes, Anne Showstack Sassoon, Sarabajaya Kumar, Ann Hudock, Carlo Borzaga, John Stewart, Paul Hirst, Grahame Thompson, Anne Phillips, Richard Levins.

Issue 5 – **Media Worlds** Bill Schwarz, James Curran, Sarah Benton, Esther Leslie, Angela McRobbie, David Hesmondhalgh, Jonathan Burston, Kevin Robins, Tony Dowmunt, Tim O'Sullivan, Phil Cohen, Duncan Green, Cynthia Cockburn

Issue 6 – **'Young Britain'** Jonathan Keane, Bilkis Malek, Elaine Pennicott, Ian Brinkley, John Healey, Frances O'Grady, Rupa Huq, Michael Kenny, Peter Gartside, Miriam Glucksmann, Costis Hadjimichalis, Joanna Moncrieff.

Issue 7 – **States of Africa** Basil Davidson, Augustin Ndahimana Buranga, Kathurima M'Inoti, Lucy Hannan, Jenny Matthews, Ngugi Wa Mirii, Kevin Watkins, Joseph Hanlon, Laurence Cockcroft, Joseph Warioba, Vic Allen, James Motlasi, Bill Schwarz, Wendy Wheeler, Dave Featherstone.

Issue 8 – **Active Welfare** Rachel Hetherington, Helen Morgan, John Pitts, Angela Leopold, Hassan Ezzedine, Alain Grevot, Margherita Gobbi, Angelo Cassin, Monica Savio, Michael Rustin, Colette Harris, Patrick Wright.

Issue 9 – **European Left** Branka Likic-Brboric, Mate Szabo, Leonadis Donskis, Peter Weinreich, Alain Caille, John Crowley, Ove Sernhede, Alexandra Alund, Angela McRobbie, Mario Petrucci, Philip Arestis, Malcolm Sawyer.

Issue 10 – **Windrush Echoes** Anne Phoenix, Jackie Kay, Julia Sudbury, Femi Franklin, David Sibley, Mike Phillips, Phil Cole, Bilkis Malek, Sonia Boyce, Roshi Naidoo, Val Wilmer and Stuart Hall, Alan Finlayson, Richard Moncrieff, Mario Pianta.

Issue 11 – **Emotional Labour** Pam Smith, Stephen Lloyd Smith, Dympna Casey, Marjorie Mayo, Minoo Moallem, Prue Chamberlayne, Rosy Martin, Sue Williams, Gillian Clarke, Andreas Hess, T. V. Sathyamurthy, Les Black, Tim Crabbe, John Solomos.

Issue 12 – Transversal Politics Nira Yuval-Davis, Pragna Patel, Marie Mulholland, Rebecca O'Rourke, Gerri Moriarty, Jane Plastow and Rosie, Bruno Latour, Gerry Hassan, Nick Jeffrey.

Issue 13 – These Sporting Times Carol Smith, Simon Cook, Adam Brown, Steve Greenfield, Guy Osborne, Gemma Bryden, Steve Hawes, Alan Tomlinson, Adam Locks, Geoff Andrews, Fred Halliday, Nick Henry, Adrian Passmore.

Issue 14 – One-Dimensional Politics Wendy Wheeler, Michael Rustin, Dave Byrne, Gavin Poynter, Barry Richards, Mario Petrucci, Ann Briggs, David Renton, Isaac Balbus, Laura Dubinsky.

Issue 15 – States of Mind Alan Shuttleworth, Andrew Cooper, Helen Lucey, Diane Reay, Richard Graham, Jennifer Wakelyn, Nancy Fraser, Stephen Wilkinson, Mike Waite, Kate Young.

Issue 16 – Civil Society Jeffrey C. Alexander, Robert Fine, Maria Pia Lara, William Outhwaite, Claire Wallace, Grazyna Kubica-Heller, Jonathan Freedland, Peter Howells, G. C. Harcourt, Emma Satyamurti, Simon Lewis, Paulette Goudge, Tom Wengraf.

Issue 17 – New Political Directions Sarah Benton, Giulio Marcon, Mario Pianta, Massimo Cacciari, Sue Tibballs, Richard Minns, Ian Taylor, John Calmore, Ruby Millington, Jon Bloomfield, Nick Henry, Phil Hubbard, Kevin Ward, David Donnison.

Issue 18 – A Very British Affair Gerry Hassan, Jim McCormick, Mark Perryman, Katie Grant, Cathal McCall, Charlotte Williams, Paul Chaney, John Coakley, Kevin Howard, Mary-Ann Stephenson, David T. Evans, Hilary Wainwright, Angie Birtill, Beatrix Campbell, Jane Foot, Csaba Deak, Geoff Andrews, Glyn Ford, Jane Desmarais.

Issue 19 - New World Disorder Stuart Hall, Chantal Mouffe, Gary Younge, Eli Zaretsky, David Slater, Bob Hackett, Jonathan Rutherford, Anne Costello, Les Levidow, Linda McDowell.

Issue 20 - Regimes of Emotion Pam Smith, Steve Smith, Arlie Russell Hochschild, Fiona Douglas, Maria Lorentzon, Gay Lee, Del Loewenthal, David Newbold, Bridget Towers, Stuart Nairn, Rick Rattue, Nelarine Cornelius, Ian Robbins, Marjorie Mayo, Trudi James, Nira Yuval Davis, Haim Bresheeth, Lena Jayyusi, Anita Biressi, Heather Nunn, Andrew Stevens, John Grieve Smith, G.C. Harcourt, Fraser Mcdonald, Andy Cumbers.

Issue 21 - Monsters and Morals Elizabeth Silva, Paul Dosh, Margrit Shildrick, Janet Fink, Dale Southerton, Caroline Knowles, Geoff Andrews, Tom Kay, Richard Minns, Steve Woodhams.

Issue 22 - Fears and Hopes Irene Bruegel, Tom Kay, Paddy Maynes, Sarah Whatmore, Steve Hinchliffe, Stuart Hall, Chantal Mouffe, Ernesto Laclau, Geoff Andrews, Stefan Howald, David Renton.

Issue 23 - Who needs history? Ali Ansari, Geoff Andrews, Kevin Morgan, Ilaria Favretto, John Callaghan, Maud Bracke, Willie Thompson, Michael Rustin, Costis Hadjimichalis, Ray Hudson, Christian Wolmar, Alan Finlayson, G.C. Harcourt, Laura Agustín.

RETHINKING SOCIAL DEMOCRACY
Conference announcement and call for papers

Rethinking Social Democracy is a series of three interdisciplinary and comparative conferences being organised to explore the past histories, present opportunities and future prospects of European social democracy.

The first conference will be in London, 15-17 April 2004, discussing Social Democracy, Culture and Society: Historical Perspectives, at the Institute of Historical Research, University of London. (For details of the other two conferences, and further information on the first, please visit the L&W website (www.lwbooks.co.uk).)

The conferences seek to contribute to debates in progress across Europe and beyond by re-evaluating the legacies of social democracy and mapping out its future prospects in view of the challenges of globalisation, the decline or retrenchment of organised labour movements and the claimed ideological hegemony of neo-liberalism. Drawing upon existing networks, the project is conceived over a sustained period as helping to make connections between academics, activists and political figures across national and disciplinary boundaries. It is the organisers' belief that it is only on an international scale, and making use of comparative methodologies, that the past achievements and limitations of European social democracy can properly be evaluated and its future world prospects clearly understood. Starting from a European perspective, we are committed to examining developments throughout the world, but particularly in places where social democratic thought and movements have been influential in the past, and also where there is clearly potential for future development.

The main focus of the first conference is the period from 1945 to the 1980s and 1990s, when post-war certainties were increasingly becoming fractured and undermined. In this period social democracy in western

Europe succeeded in challenging conservative dominance and using government power to refashion both economy and society closer to social-democratic ideals. Although these ideals came increasingly under challenge from the 1970s, the period from 1945-80 can now be seen as the golden age, not of capitalism, but of social democracy.

The conference will re-examine this golden age from a variety of perspectives - ideological, organisational, cultural and social - with a view to raising issues and setting a context for the further conferences focusing on political economy and more contemporary developments. The steering committee also welcomes papers which view this proposition from a variety of critical perspectives.

Speakers confirmed so far include: Stefano Bartolini, Alain Bergounioux, David Marquand, Ross McKibbin, Thomas Meyer, Donald Sassoon, Duncan Tanner, Giuseppe Vacca, Marcel van der Linden, Tony Wright MP.

We welcome preliminary offers of papers. Please send them by e-mail to Anne Morrow, conference administrator, anne.morrow@man.ac.uk by 10 September 2003.

Selected papers will be published as an edited collection entitled *Rethinking Social Democracy*, and in featured issues of journals, including *Socialist History*, *Soundings* and the *Journal of Southern Europe and the Balkans*.

Sponsors include the Institute of Contemporary British History; the Labour Movements group of the PSA; the Fabian Society; Manchester University International Centre for Labour Studies; New Politics Network; the Gramsci Foundation; the Office Universitaire de Recherché Socialiste (OURS); the Labour Movement Archives and Library, Stockholm; the Swedish Institute of Contemporary History; Fundació CIDOB; Fundación Alternativas; Fundació Rafael Campalans; *Soundings*, *Socialist History*, *The Journal of Southern Europe and the Balkans*; and Lawrence & Wishart.

Soundings

Described by the political theorist John Gray as a 'well written and welcome journal', Soundings is a unique venture that combines hard-edged political argument with a broad spectrum of cultural content. Recent highlights have included Stuart Hall, Jackie Kay, Gail Lewis, Mike Phillips and Lola Young on the significance of Windrush; Victoria Brittain and Basil Davidson on states of Africa; Chantal Mouffe on the third way; Angela McRobbie on the culture industries; and Bill Schwarz on the Tories; special themes have also included the European Left, Young Britain, One-Dimensional Politics and A Very British Affair.

SPECIAL OFFER TO NEW SUBSCRIBERS

First time individual subscribers are entitled to a £30 subscription for the first year

Subscription rates 2003 (3 issues)

Individual subscriptions: UK £35.00   Rest of the World £45

Institutional subscriptions: UK £70.00   Rest of the World £80.00

To subscribe, send your name and address and payment (cheque or credit card), stating which issue you want the subscription to start with, to Soundings, Lawrence and Wishart, 99a Wallis Road, London E9 5LN.

OR you can e-mail us at subscriptions@l-w-bks.demon.co.uk